THE AMAZING BASEBALL ADVENTURE

THE AMAZING BASEBALL ADVENTURE

ADVENTURE

Ballpark Wonders from the Bushes to the Show

Josh Pahigian

Guilford, Connecticut

An imprint of Globe Pequot

Distributed by NATIONAL BOOK NETWORK

British Library Cataloguing in Publication Information Available

Library of Congress Cataloging-in-Publication Data Available
ISBN 978-1-4930-2507-7 (paperback)
ISBN 978-1-4930-2508-4 (e-book)

∞™ The paper used in this publication meets the minimum requirements of American National Standard for Information Sciences—Permanence of Paper for Printed Library Materials, ANSI/NISO Z39.48-1992

Front cover photos:
Left: Photo by Dan Eidsmoe
Center: Courtesy of Tug Haines/Reading Fightin Phils
Right: Flickr Commons photo by Aaron Porzel, www.flickr.com/photos/aaronporzel/ 1364553845

Back cover photos:
Left: Photo by Ben Horne
Right: Courtesy of Brian Fleming

Top image: The Minnie and Paul sign lights up at night. Middle image: Fans fill the Green Monster seats above the American flag. Bottom Image: Logs smolder in the fire as fans watch the Great Lakes Loons game.

101 Ballpark Wonders

I was sitting beside my four-year-old son Spencer on a warm summer's night at our local minor-league baseball park. The game between the visiting New Hampshire Fisher Cats and our Portland Sea Dogs had just entered the top of the fifteenth inning and the hands on the big face clock atop the scoreboard showed five minutes to midnight. Around the twelfth inning or so, I had begun to feel a strange mixture of pride and worry. Stealing glances at Spencer sitting attentively beside me, I was delighted to think that my son shared my love of being at the ballpark, taking in its sights, participating in its rituals, sampling its cuisine, and enjoying its many other wonders. But as the crowd thinned, I realized Spencer was the only child under the age of twelve or thirteen still in attendance. His usual bedtime was 7:30 p.m.

"What do you say, Spence?" I asked after the Sea Dogs failed to score in the bottom of the tenth, eleventh, and then twelfth innings. **"Want to listen to the rest on the ride home?"**

"One more inning, Daddy," was his reply.

Yankee Stadium frieze

A ballpark wonder: Smoke billows from the bull's nostrils whenever a member of the Durham Bulls hits a home run.

"Are you sure?"

"I'm sure."

When a friendly usher stopped by our row in the middle of the thirteenth to present Spencer with a genuine game ball and remark that the game seemed like it would never end, Spencer told him, **"We're not leaving until we see the lighthouse,"** referring to the white tower that rises behind Hadlock Field's center field fence whenever a member of the Sea Dogs hits a home run or the Sea Dogs

Josh and Spencer (age three) take in a 2014 game at Hadlock Field.

win. It was our sixth or seventh game of the season already, and Spencer was still waiting. Our boys of summer had neither knocked one out of the park nor notched a W in our presence, despite Spencer's faithful insistence at each contest's outset that this would be the game.

From the Bobblehead Museum at Marlins Park

The Sea Dogs were close this night . . . just an extra-inning run away from treating us to the elusive ballpark frill hiding behind the center field fence. And so, I had let my enjoyment of the game and of my son's company override my better judgment. And now, as Sea Dogs right fielder Cole Sturgeon was preparing for his second inning of emergency relief service on the mound, the Fisher Cats' on-deck hitter was giving us a funny look through the home plate screen and stopping mid-swing to ask, **"Isn't it past your bedtime?"**

"I'm soooo tired," Spencer finally confessed.

Monument Park,
Yankee Stadium

After getting called out for suspect parenting by a twenty-two-year-old Double-A baseball player, I knew it was time to go, despite Spencer's mild protestations as I gathered up our scorebook, fifteen innings worth of souvenirs, and his sippy cup. I carried him to the car and he fell asleep clutching his baseball on the ride home, just before Sturgeon scored the winning run in the bottom of the sixteenth. As Sea Dogs broadcaster Mike Antonellis excitedly declared, "And Sturgeon crosses the plate to raise the lighthouse," I was thankful Spencer had conked out when he did.

I am happy to report that Spencer did, eventually, see the Hadlock Field lighthouse that season. Actually, he saw it just two weeks after that marathon game, when the Sea Dogs hosted the Eastern League All-Star Game, which ended in a home-run derby after both teams ran out of pitchers in extra innings. By then I had begun writing my next baseball book, the one you hold in your hands presently.

Not every baseball park has a lighthouse. In fact, just one does. And that's the point. Almost every ballpark in the majors and minors has at least one special feature that sets it apart from all the rest. Walk into practically any basketball arena, hockey rink, or football stadium and you will find it pretty similar to all the rest. But just about every baseball park presents an array of quirks that makes watching a game within its bounds a one-of-a-kind experience. Baseball's stadiums mesmerize us with their irregular field dimensions, architectural flourishes, stunning outfield views, distinctive historic markers, unique fan traditions, savory local foods, colorful characters, and other delights. This book is dedicated to celebrating these eccentricities.

The Amazing Baseball Adventure takes you on a journey to 101 of America's most amazing ballpark wonders. Like my previous baseball travel books, *101 Baseball Places to See Before You Strike Out* and *The Ultimate Baseball Road Trip*, it might serve as a practical guide that helps you plan your own baseball adventure, but it's best enjoyed as a vicarious flight of fancy that allows you to marvel at the game's most beloved ballpark features from the comfort of your easy chair.

Each spread tells the story of one ballpark flourish, exploring its history and effect on the game. Famous ballpark features like Wrigley Field's ivy, Miller Park's Sausage Race, and Durham Bulls Athletic Park's iconic snorting bull are profiled, as well as lesser-known ballpark frills like the guitar-shaped scoreboard at the home park of the Nashville Sounds, the 30-foot-tall Oil Derrick beyond the fence at the Tulsa Drillers' home park, and the stand where you can buy a delicious ballpark biscuit at the home of the Southern League's Montgomery Biscuits.

Are there more than 101 ballpark wonders across this great land of ours? Of course there are. This compilation represents only one man's catalog of baseball's special places. I fully acknowledge that although millions of us share a love of baseball, we're all individuals with our own sensibilities, so please don't hesitate to take issue with my selections or my omissions. Really, I won't be offended! I also encourage you to create your own addendum to the book, listing the ballpark attractions you deem amazing that I haven't included.

With all that said, it is my sincere hope that you enjoy this journey we're about to take together. I encourage you to bring along a friend, or perhaps a family member or two. I hope the book enriches your love of baseball and its parks. Happy reading, drive safely, eat well, and take lots of pictures! And if you ever make it to Hadlock Field, please stop by and say hello. Just don't try talking us into leaving early; Spencer's five now and informs me we won't be missing the lighthouse ever again!

Your friend and fellow traveler,

Josh Pahigian

The Big A towers over the Angel Stadium parking lot and Orange Freeway.

The iconic bull looms above the Blue Monster Wall at Durham Bulls Athletic Park. Smoke billows from its nostrils whenever the home team hits a home run.

THE SNORTING BULL AT DURHAM BULLS ATHLETIC PARK

With its slightly seedy but charming portrayal of baseball's bushes, the 1988 movie *Bull Durham* made Durham Athletic Park—with its conical ticket-house and mechanized snorting bull—a star.

Even after the real life Bulls moved to a new ballpark a mile away, the bull sign from the movie remains a vital part of the Durham baseball experience. The sign, along with the team's bull mascot, were invented by Orion Pictures. One of the most hilarious movie scenes involves Bulls pitcher Nuke Laloosh (played by Tim Robbins) finally finding his control. He retires the first five batters one night on nothing but strikes. Then, Bulls catcher Crash Davis (Kevin Costner) trots to the mound and tells him to throw the next pitch at the mascot. Nuke beans the poor sap, ensuring his opponents will think twice about digging in at the plate.

As for the snorting bull sign above the bullpen at Durham Athletic Park, it was so popular the Bulls kept it after the filming wrapped. Later, when the Bulls moved, they brought it with them, mounting it on the concourse at Durham Bulls Athletic Park. The prize attraction at the new park, however, is the even bigger bull sign atop the Fenwayesque left field wall. When the Bulls hit a homer, the 20-by-30-foot bull snorts smoke from its nostrils. Its eyes glow, too, and its tail wags. Should a homer carom off it, the hitter gets a free meal from a Durham steakhouse as the HIT BULL, WIN STEAK proclamation suggests.

The bull also comes alive when the Bulls win. So, root for the home team when you're in Durham, and if you should happen to see Annie Savoy, be sure to ask her what she thinks of the ballpark Icon Hollywood invented and then left behind in Durham.

" *Ballpark Chatter* "

Crash Davis: I want you to throw the next one at the mascot.
Nuke LaLoosh: Why? I'm finally throwing it where I want to throw it.
Crash Davis: Just throw it at the bull. Trust me.
—SCENE FROM *BULL DURHAM*

THE CRAZY HOT DOG VENDOR AT FIRSTENERGY STADIUM

Ask anyone associated with the Reading Fightin Phils, and they will tell you that Matt Jackson, graphic artist and game-day entertainment specialist, is a level-headed fellow. But when the second inning rolls around at FirstEnergy Stadium, Jackson becomes an ostrich-riding lunatic named Frank Furter. "The Crazy Hot Dog Vendor" rides around the infield on his faithful ostrich Rodrigo firing tin-foil-wrapped hot dogs into the stands with his right hand, while attempting to tame Rodrigo with the tether in his left hand. Fans cheer and players hold their gloves to their mouths to hide their laughter.

With his thick-rimmed glasses, red bowtie, mop of hair, red pinstriped vest, paper hat, and white pants, shirt, and wristbands, the Crazy Hot Dog Vendor is perhaps the least likely between-inning superstar to ever stride onto a professional baseball field. But ever since his first venture onto the Reading lawn in 2004, he has been a rock star.

Jackson dreamt up the character in 2003 after a barnstorming funnyman known as Roscoe De Vendor failed to show up at FirstEnergy Stadium for a scheduled appearance due to a traveling mishap. Jackson studied a photo of the faux vendor and let himself imagine what it would be like to don similar garb and act crazy on the field. During the offseason, the Reading front office pitched the idea to one of its sponsors, Berks Packing Company. Berks bit! At first, fans didn't know what to make of Jackson's act, but before long it had become a daily highlight of the "Baseballtown" experience.

The Crazy Hot Dog Vendor has even reshaped Reading's brand. In 2013, the "Reading Phillies" became the Fightin Phils and adopted logos of a feathery R and an ostrich putting up its dukes.

" *Ballpark Chatter* "

"It's great to see the smallest kids' faces who think it's real, to the grandparents who just want a high five. I always read a Joe DiMaggio quote before I run out there: 'This could be some kid's first time seeing me or some fan's last time. I owe them my best.'"

—MATT JACKSON, AKA "THE CRAZY HOT DOG VENDOR"

The Crazy Hot Dog Vendor,
his satchel of hot dogs,
and his ostrich—Rodrigo

Three sausage races with three leaders—the Polish, the Italian, and the Chorizo

THE SAUSAGE RACE AT MILLER PARK

I n the land of brews and brats, where fans sing "Roll Out the Barrel" in the middle of the seventh inning, and toast Bernie Brewer, the ballpark frill that really brings fans to their feet is the daily Sausage Race. The middle-of-the-sixth-inning sprint features colorfully costumed Bratwurst, Polish, Italian, Hot Dog, and Chorizo sausages racing down the left field line and around the bend behind home plate.

When the race began, it didn't include personified meat products, but rather black and white cartoon sausages racing on the County Stadium video board. The three initial contestants (Bratwurst, Polish, and Italian) whizzed past familiar Milwaukee landmarks on their way to the ballpark. All that changed on a summer Sunday in 1993, though, when the race began and appeared to have concluded in its usual way, until, suddenly, a gate swung open on the left field wall and three 8-foot-tall sausages raced onto the field. The surprised fans went crazy, while the players and umpires looked on with a mixture of amusement and horror. It *was* pretty funny, but some baseball insiders said afterward that it had made a mockery of the game. It wouldn't be long, though, before the guardians of the game got on board.

The idea to stage an actual mascot race on the field came from a man named Michael Dillon. Dillon made the costumes for the first race himself and enlisted two friends to run on the field with him. After the racing sausages created such a sizzle that day, the Brewers brought them back for select games during the remainder of the 1993 season. The next season, Klement's Sausage Company signed on as the race's sponsor, and the race remains the highlight of the Milwaukee ballpark experience to this day.

MILLER PARK

- Find the **Bob Uecker statue** in the upper level seats behind home plate
- Cheer for **Bernie Brewer** as he mounts his outfield slide
- Eat a **bratwurst** with **Secret Stadium Sauce**

BALLPARK BUCKET LIST

★ MAX PATKIN ★
THE CLOWN PRINCE OF BASEBALL

White Sox minor leaguer Max Patkin never sniffed the big leagues before heading off to serve in World War II. Then, on a military base in Hawaii, Patkin started goofing on Joe DiMaggio after serving up a long home run to the Yankee slugger . . . and the crowd went wild. After the war, Patkin reinvented himself as "The Clown Prince of Baseball," serving as the mascot for dozens of major- and minor-league teams over the next five decades.

IN BASEBALL HISTORY

- No less a baseball visionary than Bill Veeck discovered Patkin. Veeck hired Patkin recurrently as "coach" for his Browns, Indians, and White Sox.
- In between stints for Veeck, Patkin barnstormed the country, entertaining fans at minor-league parks.
- Patkin's most famous routines included mimicking a first baseman tossing warmup balls around the infield, giving fake signs to opposing players, shadowing players around the bases after home runs, and digging in at the plate for mimed at-bats.
- With his elastic face, toothless grin, and tilted cap, Patkin was one of the minor leagues' most recognizable figures from the 1940s through 1980s, when he made more than 4,000 appearances.
- Patkin played himself in the classic baseball film *Bull Durham*.

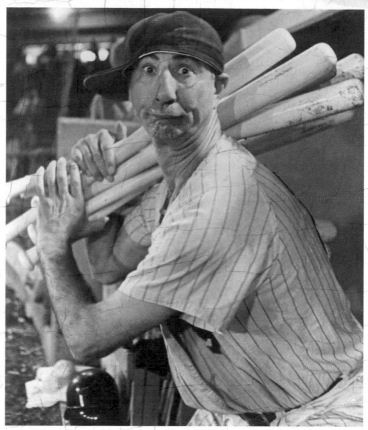

Boston Red Sox
THE GREEN MONSTER AT FENWAY PARK

Fenway Park's left field wall, the Green Monster, was raised in the wake of a fire that destroyed the left field grandstand and center field bleachers on January 5, 1934. In place of "Duffy's Cliff," a bluff that Red Sox left fielder Duffy Lewis had become expert in scaling, and the 25-foot-high fence that had stood atop it, fans found a level playing field backed by a 37-foot, 2-inch wall designed to keep balls from flying onto Lansdowne Street. Since 2003, fans have also found four rows of Green Monster Seats offering bird's-eye views of the field at the very top.

On the face of the Monster, you find a ladder from the era when attendants scaled the wall to retrieve balls from a net that once ran high above the field. The slate scoreboard's sections display the line score of the current game, the American League East standings, and the out-of-town American and National League scores, all thanks to three attendants hoisting 13-by-16-inch, 2-pound slate tiles into slots. The only electronic components are beneath the line score—dot-matrix numerals for the batter's uniform number, and red and green lights indicating the count on the batter, number of outs, and hit (H) or error (E).

The green paint was slathered in 1947. Previously, the Monster hosted billboards for products from shaving razors to whiskey. In those earlier days, players like Ted Williams and Jimmy Piersall began the tradition—continued to this day—of stepping into the scoreboard through its small door to sign the concrete base of Fenway Park.

The most famous Green Monster moment was Carlton Fisk's twelfth-inning home run off the foul pole to win Game Six of the 1975 World Series. NBC Sports famously captured Fisk waving the ball fair as he hopped along the first base line.

FULL COUNT

127 Slots on the Green Monster's manually operated scoreboard

The Green Monster up close, at twilight, and draped with the American flag before Game One of the 2013 World Series

The San Diego Chicken bites a fan at Petco Park, parades his "baby chicks" during a game, and holds up an eye chart for the benefit of MLB umpire Rob Drake.

THE SAN DIEGO CHICKEN

In 1974 twenty-year-old San Diego State University student Ted Giannoulas took a part-time job wearing a chicken suit at the San Diego Zoo before Easter. KGB-Radio was hanging billboards across San Diego featuring a cartoon chicken nesting on two eggs that represented its AM and FM stations, and Giannoulas was charged with doling out plastic eggs to remind San Diegans of the promotion. For his efforts, he was paid two dollars an hour.

After thoroughly enjoying the gig, Giannoulas proposed wearing the chicken suit to the Padres' home opener at San Diego Stadium, and KGB agreed. From the start, the laid-back San Diego fans ate up the Chicken's act. He heckled umpires, flapped his feathers in opposing players' faces, stomped atop the dugout roofs, and provided welcomed comic relief during some lean times for the Friars. By 1976, he was ready to spread his wings and fly, and after a group of St. Louis Cardinals players pooled their money and arranged for him to visit the Gateway City, he did just that, playing two games at Busch Stadium.

Realizing Giannoulas had struck gold, KGB filed a lawsuit against him, claiming it owned the rights to the Chicken. After Giannoulas was stripped of his feathers, the fans chased an imposter chicken from the San Diego Stadium stands, and the radio station faced a blistering public backlash. Finally, Giannoulas had his day in court and won in June of 1979. He made a triumphant return to San Diego Stadium riding in a giant foam egg that was escorted by a California Highway Patrol motorcade.

Before long, Giannoulas was appearing at ballparks and arenas across the country again. Today, he makes about fifty appearances annually at minor-league parks across America.

" *Ballpark Chatter* "

"The Chicken has the soul of a poet. He is an embryonic Charles Chaplin in chicken feathers."

—JACK MURPHY, *SAN DIEGO UNION* SPORTSWRITER

6 *Chicago Cubs*

THE IVY AT WRIGLEY FIELD

There is perhaps no more beautiful ballpark flourish than the veil of ivy on the 11-foot, 6-inch outfield wall at Wrigley Field. The brainchild of baseball visionary Bill Veeck, the ivy creates a rustic backdrop for games played beneath Chicago's urban landscape.

Although baseball myth proclaims that Veeck himself planted the vines—largely because Veeck's autobiography says so—historical evidence suggests he pitched the idea to Cubs owner Philip K. Wrigley and then contracted the work to a local nursery. Whoever pressed the vines into the dirt planted a quick-growing strain called Bittersweet ivy and a robust and enduring strain called Boston ivy. And by season's end the Bittersweet was already racing up the brick wall that had only recently replaced a wooden fence.

The ivy affects the way games at Wrigley are played too. Outfielders have to think twice about racing too aggressively onto the warning track. While the ivy may provide some slight cushion to ball hawks who run into the brick wall, by today's standards it offers little protection from injury.

The ivy also swallows long hits, turning them into ground-rule doubles. Sometimes the ivy spits out balls; other times it sucks them in. On hits to the base of the wall, outfielders must make a snap decision: raise their hands to signal a ball is lost in the curtain of green, or attempt to recoup the ball and return it to the infield. But if an outfielder attempts to retrieve a ball from the vines before he signals that it's lost, or if he fails to retrieve a ball that the nearest umpire deems insufficiently ensconced, he may not get the ground-rule double call. The ump might say the ball is still in play, and while the fielder is holding his hands in the air, the batter might scamper all the way to third or even home.

FULL COUNT

550 Vines of Bittersweet and Boston ivy planted in 1937

Ivy surrounds the 400-foot marker
on the center field wall.

The species of the Phillie Phanatic has remained a mystery for more than four decades.

THE PHILLIE PHANATIC AT CITIZENS BANK PARK

Zooming around Citizens Bank Park on a four-wheeler, the Phillie Phanatic terrorizes opposing players during the pregame hour, and then spends the game ambling through the stands wiping his brow with visiting fans' hats, shining bald heads, and taking bites out of fans' cotton candy. He has been known to dump popcorn on fans who irk him and to shoot Silly String at players.

He stands 6-feet, 6-inches tall and weighs 300 pounds. He wears a Phillies jersey with a red star on back. His eyelashes are purple. His legs are red. And his nose is an inverted green horn.

The Phanatic was dreamt up by a Brooklyn marketing company in 1978 after the Phillies observed the growing popularity of the San Diego Chicken. After commissioning the project, Phillies vice president Bill Giles was presented the choice of buying the Phanatic costume for $3,900 or buying the costume *and the copyright* to it for $5,200. Giles decided to save a few bucks, leaving Harrison/Erickson the owner of the copyright. A few years later, Giles led a group of investors that bought the Phillies, and as part of the deal they paid a quarter-million dollars to Harrison/Erickson for full rights.

The Phanatic's finest hour may have come in 1988, when he dressed a mannequin in a Dodgers jersey and stuffed its belly with T-shirts. He threw the Tommy Lasorda effigy onto the field and stomped on it in front of the Dodgers dugout. The enraged skipper burst onto the field and threw the Phanatic to the ground, then picked up the mannequin and beat the Phanatic about the head with it. As the Phanatic finally mounted his four-wheeler, he took one last parting shot, sticking out his belly in mockery of Lasorda's rotund physique.

" *Ballpark Chatter* "

"My barber knows who I am, and sometimes I'll go in for a haircut and he'll say things to his customers like, 'Did you see what the Phanatic did last night? Wasn't that something?' And I'll just sit there and smile and try to keep quiet."

—TOM BURGOYNE, THE MAN INSIDE THE PHILLIE PHANATIC SUIT SINCE 1994

8 New York Yankees

THE FRIEZE AT YANKEE STADIUM

With origins that date to the opening of the original "House That Ruth Built" in 1923, the Yankee Stadium frieze has been the signature feature of all three incarnations of the Yankees' home. It is amazing to think that this fancy white metalwork has been part of the Grand Old Game even longer than Boston's iconic left field wall or Chicago's ivy.

Visiting the Bronx today, you find the white steel slats forming a continuous structure that looks something like an upside-down picket fence. The frieze provides the mustard atop the hot dog without which the new Yankee Stadium would have never felt complete.

It is unclear whether former Yankees owner Jacob Ruppert or the stadium's architects dreamt up the frieze, but it did follow in the tradition of the ironwork at the Yankees' former home, the Polo Grounds.

In its original form, the frieze topped the entire upper deck at Yankee Stadium, appearing on the face of the sunroof where it does today. This was the frieze off which Mickey Mantle clanked the longest home run in Yankee Stadium history, an eleventh inning walk-off shot against Kansas City in 1963.

At the second version of Yankee Stadium, which stood from 1976 to 2008, the frieze could only be found above the outfield bleachers, while track lighting appeared atop the sunroof of the upper deck. Today's more prominent frieze takes the form of white zinc-coated steel. It hangs down 12 feet from the roof, and weighs 315 tons. And you might have wondered how the Yankees racked up a $1.5 billion bill in constructing their new home?

Mounted atop this white adornment, you find the barely noticeable stadium lights, which are more attractive than the light banks on metal stanchions at most parks. Higher still, you find the colorful pennants of all the big league clubs.

YANKEE STADIUM

- Grab a beverage at **Stan's Sports Bar**, the quintessential Yankee fan hangout
- Stroll the **Yankees Timeline** on the first-level concourse
- Wander the **Great Hall**, inside the main gates, with its towering portraits of Babe Ruth, Joe DiMaggio, Derek Jeter, and other Yankee legends

BALLPARK BUCKET LIST

The iconic white frieze adorns Yankee Stadium's top level, where fans sitting there enjoy a close-up view.

The view from across the Allegheny River, and a sunset on the Clemente Bridge

THE ROBERTO CLEMENTE BRIDGE AT PNC PARK

When it came time for Pittsburgh to replace Three Rivers Stadium, a groundswell of support arose to name the new baseball park after Pirates legend Roberto Clemente. Instead, the diamond was named after a bank. But Clemente admirers were granted the considerable consolation prize of a bridge renamed in their hero's honor . . . and not just any bridge, but one that would become the new park's signature feature. As the sun sets on the Steel City's downtown high-rises, the yellow bridge glows with special meaning.

Known as the Sixth Street Bridge prior to its rechristening in 1998, the bridge is one of three yellow suspension bridges that cross the Allegheny River in downtown Pittsburgh. The Andy Warhol Bridge and Rachel Carson Bridge are the others.

Walking across the Clemente Bridge after parking in a downtown garage or exiting the Wood Street light rail station on game day, you encounter street vendors lining its 884-foot expanse as well as several historic markers. One of the plaques honors the Allegheny County Public Works employees who built the bridge in 1927 and 1928; another crowns the bridge a National Historic Landmark; and, most interestingly to baseball fans, another reads ROBERTO in big letters, while also displaying the years of Clemente's birth (1934) and premature death (1972), a bronze bust of him, and the words:

> WITH HIS PASSIONATE HEART AND GOD-GIVEN ABILITIES, HE LIVED HIS LIFE LIKE HE PLAYED THE GAME. HE HELPED HIS PIRATES WIN AND HIS FELLOW MAN OVERCOME . . . ROBERTO WILL ALWAYS BE REMEMBERED AS PITTSBURGH'S ADOPTED SON. THANKS, GREAT ONE.

After traversing this unique ballpark runway, you arrive at a 12-foot-tall statue of Clemente outside PNC Park. Then, you settle into your ballpark seat to find baseball's most beloved bridge in your field of sight.

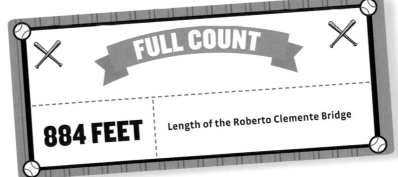

FULL COUNT

884 FEET Length of the Roberto Clemente Bridge

10 *Nashville Sounds*

THE GUITAR SCOREBOARD AT FIRST TENNESSEE PARK

In the land of the Grand Ole Opry, live music clubs, and record companies, the local minor leaguers play in the shadows of a giant guitar. No matter where you sit at Nashville's First Tennessee Park, you can't help but look at the big instrument all game long. What's the count? Where does this guy bat in the lineup? How many innings until they start launching those postgame fireworks? The guitar will tell you. Each glance at the Sounds' guitar-shaped scoreboard reminds you that you're in Music City.

When the game is in progress, the guitar usually displays the batter's headshot on the top half of its body, with his stats, and his team's batting lineup below. It can also display animations, instant replays, and pretty much whatever else the folks in the press box think would enhance your enjoyment of the game. The neck shows the line score, with each fret "framing" an inning. The head serves as its own little high-definition board, providing further information about the batter or pitcher, or serving as a giant clock. Altogether, the board measures 144 feet long by 55 feet tall.

This version of the guitar was unveiled on April 17, 2015 when the Sounds opened brand new First Tennessee Park on the grounds where Nashville's mythic Sulphur Dell once stood. Before moving to First Tennessee Park, the Sounds had played at Herschel Greer Stadium, where the first version of the big guitar—the brainchild of former team owner Larry Schmittou—was raised in 1993. The original guitar displayed the time and temperature on its body along with lots of advertising, as well as the line score on its neck; a beer company logo adorned all its tuning pegs. And whenever a player cranked a home run off the board, he was presented a free guitar courtesy of a local music store.

" *Ballpark Chatter* "

"We listen to our fans. Keeping the beloved guitar-shaped scoreboard is just part of our commitment to our supporters and to the city of Nashville. . . . And we will continue to have the most talked-about scoreboard in baseball."

—SOUNDS OWNER FRANK WARD, ANNOUNCING THE GUITAR SCOREBOARD WOULD BE RECREATED AT FIRST TENNESSEE PARK

The guitar-shaped scoreboard looming over right field is modeled after the original Sounds' scoreboard from their previous home, Greer Stadium.

Honest Abe always runs the Presidents Race fair and square as he competes against foes like Teddy Roosevelt— out to an early lead in this action shot.

THE RACING PRESIDENTS AT NATIONALS PARK

After the visiting team takes its hacks in the top of the fourth inning at Nationals Park, a gaggle of former US presidents comes bumbling onto the center field warning track and then heads toward the right field line before hanging a right and streaking toward the infield.

The Presidents Race began in cartoon form at the Nationals' original home, RFK Stadium, in 2005. It is similar, of course, to the midgame mascot races in other cities, but deserves credit for being the goofiest jaunt of all. You just can't beat the ridiculousness of watching the most dignified men in our nation's history depicted in bobble-headed caricature, bumping into one another, falling on their faces, and otherwise jostling for position.

One of the neatest things about the race is the way it presents its own subplots over the course of each season or over several seasons . . . as Teddy Roosevelt—of the 525-race losing streak—would surely attest! For nearly seven full seasons, Teddy ran . . . and lost . . . game after game. Finally, on the afternoon of the 2012 regular season finale, he claimed his first win when an imitation Phillie Phanatic jumped onto the field and knocked over Presidents Washington, Lincoln, and Jefferson. That postseason, Teddy won three races during the Nationals first-ever playoff series, a five-game Division Series defeat to the St. Louis Cardinals.

Eventually, the field expanded to six racers with the additions of William Howard Taft in 2013 and Calvin Coolidge in 2015. Coolidge, who was dubbed a "visiting racer" from the start, was replaced by Herbert Hoover in 2016.

FULL COUNT

525 | Consecutive races lost by Teddy Roosevelt before winning three in a row

12 New York Mets

THE JACKIE ROBINSON ROTUNDA AT CITI FIELD

Once upon a time, Brooklyn Dodgers fans passed through a classy home plate rotunda to enter Ebbets Field. The famous rotunda had 80-foot ceilings, a marble floor, an ornate baseball bat chandelier, and baseball light fixtures. Nearly half a century later, when the New York Mets replaced Shea Stadium with a new ballpark, Mets owner Fred Wilpon decided to recreate the rotunda he had known as a child and to use it as a place to honor the greatest Brooklyn Dodger of all, Jackie Robinson.

Sure, it is unusual to honor another franchise's most famous player at your ballpark, but this is the one case in which it makes perfect sense. After all, not only did Robinson play in nearby Brooklyn, but he transcended his status as a Dodgers legend to become a legend of the game. Indeed, his breaking baseball's color barrier changed the game forever . . . in every city.

The Jackie Robinson Rotunda was dedicated on April 15, 2009, the date of Major League Baseball's annual Jackie Robinson Day. Upon entering it, you encounter an 8-foot-tall blue sculpture of Robinson's No. 42, which is retired throughout the game. Pictures of Robinson adorn the walls, including ones of him with his wife Rachel, Dodgers general manager Branch Rickey, and Dodgers teammates.

Atop the upper level, you find the same quote that appears on Robinson's grave at Cypress Hills Cemetery in Brooklyn, declaring, "A life is not important except in the impact it has on other lives."

At your feet, you find the qualities Robinson exhibited—courage, persistence, excellence, citizenship, determination, etc.—etched into the Italian marble floor with text describing how he demonstrated each characteristic.

 Ballpark Chatter

"A life is not important except in the impact it has on other lives."

—JACKIE ROBINSON

The Jackie Robinson Rotunda, with the memorial inside, recreates the grandeur of the rotunda that once welcomed fans to Ebbets Field.

Jackie Robinson's universally retired No. 42 joins the Yankees other retired numbers, including those of Andy Pettitte, Jorge Posada, and Bernie Williams, which were all added to Monument Park in 2015.

MONUMENT PARK AT YANKEE STADIUM

After an unspectacular playing career, second baseman Miller Huggins earned a lasting place in the annals of the Grand Old Game as a manager, leading the upstart Yankees to six American League pennants and three world championships over a twelve-year span that began in 1918. With Huggins at the helm, the Yanks turned former Red Sox southpaw Babe Ruth into an everyday outfielder, built Yankee Stadium, and won their first World Series, laying the foundation for a professional sports juggernaut that stands unrivaled to this day. The only thing that could end Huggins's run was his premature death at age fifty from blood poisoning. From his tragic loss, a ballpark landmark was born, one we still find at today's third incarnation of Yankee Stadium. We're talking, of course, about Monument Park.

In its earliest days, this special parcel housed a single slab of granite bearing a bronze engraving to honor Huggins. Installed in 1932, the memorial resided on the field of play near the Yankee Stadium flagpole some 490 feet from home plate. The Yankees added a second monument in 1941 to honor Lou Gehrig, whose life was similarly cut short by illness, then another in 1948 after Ruth died of cancer. Out of these losses, Monument Park had sprouted, only it wasn't called Monument Park until after Yankee Stadium was rebuilt during the 1974 and 1975 seasons.

At today's Yankee Stadium, you find the three original monuments, as well as ones honoring Mickey Mantle, Joe DiMaggio, George Steinbrenner, and dozens of plaques honoring lesser Yankee lights. The park also displays the retired numbers of those Yankees whose jerseys shan't ever be donned again.

YANKEE STADIUM'S MONUMENT PARK

- Find the **monument** honoring the victims of the September 11, 2001, terrorist attacks

- Find the **plaques** commemorating the masses three popes have celebrated at Yankee Stadium

- Find the **two retired No. 8s**, one for Yogi Berra and one for fellow catcher Bill Dickey

BALLPARK BUCKET LIST

14 *Dayton Dragons*

THE SMOKING DRAGONS AT FIFTH THIRD FIELD

To figure out why the Dayton Dragons lead the Midwest League in attendance year in and year out, you needn't look much farther than their ballpark, which absolutely oozes fun. And the highlight of any trip to Fifth Third Field is the video board in left-center field that comes to life when the home team has reason to celebrate. Actually, the board itself doesn't come to life; the 20-foot-tall dragons on either side of it do. Smoke billows from their nostrils and their eyes glow red.

In 2000, which just happened to be the Chinese Year of the Dragon, the Rockford Reds moved to Dayton and underwent a rebranding. The other Midwest League franchises had logical enough names that tied them to their cities' agricultural, industrial, or geographic reputations, and Dayton wanted something different. "Dragons" had not been overused in American sports and was alliterative when paired with the D in Dayton. So the club contracted a graphic artist to come up with a logo, and then staged a name-revealing party for fans in downtown Dayton that included some costumed dragons and knights.

Of course, no one could have predicted at the time that the Harry Potter series and television show *Game of Thrones* would bring dragons into the American mainstream over the coming decades. To be sure, dragons are hot right now, and in no place is that truer than Dayton, where the local Midwest League team can't print tickets or stamp logos onto T-shirts fast enough to meet the demand. Fifth Third Field's signature feature—its dragon scoreboard—is a fitting representation of the team's resounding success.

FULL COUNT

1,188 Consecutive Dayton Dragons sellouts through 2016, an all-time North American sports record

The dragons keep an eye on the game while guarding the Fifth Third Field Scoreboard.

A view of the fountain's show during the seventh-inning stretch, and a view of the field from behind the fountain

THE WATER SPECTACULAR AT KAUFFMAN STADIUM

The Midwest's self-proclaimed "City of Fountains" boasts approximately 200 of the manmade geysers, more than any city in the world besides Rome. Fittingly, the Royals' Water Spectacular has become one of baseball's most recognizable ballpark attractions over the past half-century.

Designed and funded by Royals founder Ewing M. Kauffman, the breathtaking display spans 322 feet, beginning high above the right field fence and continuing to left-center. It circulates more than a half million gallons of water through its pools on three levels, treating you to cascading waterfalls all game long. The fountain also comes to life between innings, shooting LED-lighted spouts into the air.

While the fountain has been Kauffman Stadium's signature feature since the park's opening in 1973, it was made even more prominent by a 2009 renovation that added new seats and standing areas across the outfield that enable you to watch the game from the fountain's midst, or mist, if you will.

Just don't get the wrong idea; while outfield swimming is allowed at some parks, it is prohibited in Kansas City. In August 2013, a female fan found this out the hard way. With the Royals cruising toward a 13–0 win over the Twins, the twenty-five-year-old made the ill-conceived decision to take a dip in the left field waters. For several minutes she led ballpark security on a multi-pool chase while the game continued until she was finally captured in the center field stands. "The Fountain Lady," as she was dubbed by viral YouTube posts, was arrested and spent the night in jail. The moral of the story? Leave your swim trunks at home and be content to enjoy the most beautiful manmade attraction in the big leagues from your ballpark seat.

" Ballpark Chatter "

"Anybody who goes into the fountains is an automatic arrest and taken into Kansas City, Missouri, police custody and to jail, where they have to post bond."

—TOBY COOK, KANSAS CITY ROYALS SPOKESPERSON, AFTER A FAN JUMPED INTO THE FOUNTAIN DURING THE 2014 ROYALS PLAYOFF RUN

Blast from the Past!

★ HOT PANTS DAY ★
OAKLAND A'S, JUNE 27, 1971

After moving his A's from Kansas City to Oakland in 1968, Charlie O. Finley made his mark as one of the game's most flamboyant promoters. His teams were also highly successful. While their owner experimented with orange balls and staged outrageous promotions, the A's won three straight World Series from 1972 to 1974. On "Hot Pants Day," more than 6,000 women received free admission to the A's doubleheader against the Royals, and between games paraded on the field for a fashion show.

BASEBALL HISTORY IN THE DAYS OF DISCO

- Despite winning the AL West title with a 101-60 record, the 1971 A's ranked eighteenth among MLB's twenty-four teams in attendance, drawing only 915,000 fans.
- In 1971, *All in the Family* was America's top TV show, the Bee Gees were emerging cultural icons, and Richard Nixon was the *Time* magazine "Man of the Year."
- After Charlie Finley hired Stanley Burrell to serve as batboy at Oakland-Alameda County Coliseum, Reggie Jackson nicknamed the teen "Hammer" due to his resemblance to Hank Aaron. Burrell would later achieve pop fame as "MC Hammer."

16 At a Ballpark Near You

THE ZOOPERSTARS!

If you find that your home team's usual between-inning stunts are starting to feel a little stale, you should circle the date on their calendar when the ZOOperstars! are coming to town. The barnstorming baseball pranksters fill the lulls in the action with an array of sights you've likely never before seen on a professional field of play. Ten-foot-tall bivalves Roger Clamens and Clammy Sosa devour unsuspecting groundskeepers, umpires, and third base coaches. The muscle-bound Alex Frogriguez challenges members of the home team to a dance-off and then pulls down their pants when they start dancing. Centipete Rose breaks into pieces and frantically tries to put himself back together. And the alter-ego of longtime Chicago Cubs broadcaster Harry Caray, Harry Canary, ambles into the stands in the middle of the seventh inning to lead fans in the traditional singing of "Take Me Out to the Ballgame."

Created by brothers Dominic and Brennan Latkovski in the 1990s, the ZOOperstars! consist of more than twenty men and women who travel North America performing skits like these in different player-themed parody costumes. During the course of a typical baseball season, they put on more than a hundred shows at different minor-league parks.

The story of how the Latkovskis broke into the ballpark promotions business dates to the late 1980s and early 1990s when Dominic spent four summers portraying Billy Bird, the mascot for the Triple-A Louisville Redbirds. In 1991, Louisville hosted the Triple-A All-Star Game and Billy Bird caught the attention of some of the minor leagues' movers and shakers. The next season, the Latkovskis rented a booth at the Minor League Baseball Trade Show and booked fifty gigs across the country for their act, which evolved from Billy Bird & Company to BirdZerk! in 1995. The success of those characters led to the creation of the ZOOperstars!

FULL COUNT

10 MILLION — Social media shares of the ZOOperstars! Famous "Eat It" routine

The ZOOperstars at Wrigley Field, including Clammy Sosa, Harry Canary, Monkey Mantle, Ken Giraffey Jr., and Whale Gretzky

Fans sun themselves in the right field pavilion during a 2014 game, and Clayton Kershaw pitches with the wavy pavilion roof and looming hillside behind him.

THE WAVY ROOFS AT DODGER STADIUM

High above the City of Angels, construction workers began digging into a Los Angeles peak known as Lookout Mountain in 1959. By the time they were done carting away more than 8 million cubic yards of earth, the workers had laid the foundation for the first multi-level big-league park built without the need for those view-blocking support pillars East Coast fans had been cursing for generations. More than that, they had created an idyllic ball field in the sky that showcased the most beautiful outfield view in baseball, one that treated spectators to the purple peaks of the San Gabriel Mountains. Since its inception, Dodger Stadium's design has also reflected the ups and downs of its surroundings. The wavy roofs atop the stadium's outfield pavilions mimic the zigzagging natural landscape and provide the stadium's signature feature.

Although the Dodgers have renovated Dodger Stadium fairly extensively in recent years, the work hasn't touched the pavilion roofs, despite the fact that the lids serve little functional purpose, providing only slight sun-relief due to the park's orientation. And it hardly ever rains in Los Angeles—the Dodgers carried an MLB-record streak of 1,293 home games without a rainout into 2016. The roofs are adornments for adornments' sake and darned good ones.

If you aim for a seat behind home plate—no matter the seating level—you enjoy the delightful backdrop for a game the wavy roofs create. Counterintuitive though it may seem, the upper deck treats you to the best view of all, one that presents the perfect unity of the rising and falling roofs, the looming hills, and distant mountains. This delightful composition creates a game-day backdrop that even George Lucas, J. J. Abrams, and the rest of the fantasyland studio whizzes would find hard to top!

DODGER STADIUM

- Check out the larger-than-life **Dodgers bobbleheads** adorning the stadium grounds
- Catch a bag of **peanuts** from Roger Owens, the legendary vendor who has been working Dodgers games since back when they played at the Los Angeles Memorial Coliseum
- Order a **Meatball Marinara Cone**—a meatball in an ice-cream cone-shaped roll—from Tommy Lasorda's Trattoria on the right field concourse

BALLPARK BUCKET LIST

18 *Albuquerque Isotopes*

THE SIMPSONS STATUES AT ISOTOPES PARK

The story of how life-size statues of Homer, Marge, Bart, and Lisa Simpson came to reside on the Isotopes Park concourse is as colorful as the statues themselves.

A 1990 episode of *The Simpsons* titled "Dancing Homer" portrayed the family enjoying a Springfield Isotopes game at Duff Stadium. After the video board beamed the image of Homer dancing in the stands, he became a crowd favorite and was soon after anointed team mascot . . . and the hijinks and hilarity ensued.

More than a decade later, "Hungry, Hungry Homer" depicted the Isotopes secretly planning to depart Springfield for a new ballpark in Albuquerque. In protest, Homer chained himself to Duff Stadium and began a hunger strike to prevent the "Albuquerque Isotopes" from becoming a (fictional) reality.

When that second episode ran in 2001, Albuquerque had just lost its team, the Dukes, and was, in fact, courting teams seeking better digs than their home cities were presently offering.

Two years later, the Duke City enticed the Calgary Cannons to relocate with the promise of a thoroughly renovated stadium. Prior to the franchise's arrival, a name-the-team poll was put before readers of the *Albuquerque Tribune*. The newspaper offered Dukes, Atoms, 66ers, Roadrunners, and Isotopes as choices. Nearly two-thirds of the 120,000 respondents picked Isotopes in homage to the familiar *Simpsons* episodes.

In October 2009, Isotopes general manager John Traub was in Los Angeles to watch the Dodgers' 2009 playoff series against the St. Louis Cardinals, when he stumbled upon a set of Homer and Marge figures—originally created as advertising props for *The Simpsons Movie*—at an antique shop. And so, Homer and Marge made the trip east, underwent a thorough refurbishing, and were installed at Isotopes Park in time for Opening Day 2010. Statues of Lisa and Bart were added a couple of seasons later.

" *Ballpark Chatter* "

Lisa Simpson: There's just the green grass of the outfield, the crushed brick of the infield, and the white chalk lines that divide the man from the little boy.
Homer Simpson: Lisa, honey. You're forgetting the beer. It comes in 72-ounce tubs here.

—*THE SIMPSONS*, "DANCING HOMER" EPISODE

Homer Simpson ready for the game, and posing with members of the Mile High Little League

The Mets' current Home Run Apple, and the original apple from Shea Stadium that now sits outside Citi Field's main entrance

THE HOME RUN APPLE AT CITI FIELD

The Citi Field Home Run Apple waits behind the center field fence for a member of the Mets to homer, then rises in celebration.

This unique Mets tradition dates to 1980 when an earlier version of the apple first appeared at Shea Stadium. Today's bigger, badder apple takes about five seconds to rise 15 feet. LED lights trace the Mets logo on its red fiberglass skin, while the fans cheer, and the vanquishing player circles the bases.

The apple was born at a time when the euphoria of the Mets' amazing 1969 season had begun to fade. Sensing the team was lacking that extra something (namely talent), the Mets launched a PR campaign around the idea that the latest bunch of unlikely heroes might channel the spirit of the club Tom Seaver had led to October glory. They came up with the slogan "The Magic is Back," and installed an upside-down top hat behind the outfield fence with an apple inside. The hat was a nod to the drawing baseball commissioner Spike Eckert orchestrated in 1966 that awarded Seaver to the Mets after Eckert voided his contract with the Braves on the grounds that they had signed their No. 1 pick too late.

Before long, the Mets' fortunes turned, and their fans came to love the apple. When the Mets began plotting a move to a new park in the 2000s, fans implored the team to save the apple from the compost heap, and the team did. Visiting Citi Field today, you will find the old apple planted outside Citi Field's main entrance. And, even when the Mets don't homer, you enjoy at least one appearance from the new apple per game, as it rises daily during the seventh-inning stretch.

CITI FIELD

- Take a lap around the **Shea Stadium bases** in the Citi Field parking lot

- Visit the **Mets Hall of Fame and Museum** with its statue of the baseball-headed Mr. Met

- Sing along with **"Meet the Mets"** when it plays between innings

BALLPARK BUCKET LIST

L.A. Angels of Anaheim

THE BIG A AT ANGEL STADIUM OF ANAHEIM

Rarely do you encounter a landmark so visionary, unique, and . . . well . . . enormous . . . that it transcends the bounds of its ballpark. But visiting Anaheim, whether you are a motorist passing by on the 57 or a baseball road-tripper pulling into the Angel Stadium parking lot, you can't miss the iconic tower with the golden halo.

Today, the Big A is located at the far end of the stadium parking lot, but when Anaheim Stadium first opened in 1966, it rose right behind the left field fence, supporting the ballpark scoreboard and various advertising signs. Back then it was white instead of red. Standing higher than the ballpark light towers, it awaited long balls to left that would clank off its scoreboard or fly through its opening and into the parking lot.

A 1980 renovation to retrofit the stadium for football relocated the Big A more than a thousand feet to its present location on the right field side of the stadium. This, to make way for football stands across the outfield so the NFL's Rams could join the Angels as co-tenants.

The Rams eventually departed for St. Louis in 1995, clearing the way for another renovation to open up the outfield. But you still can't see the Big A from most locations within the park. It is more visible to motorists passing outside, though, than it used to be, and when the Angels win—whether home or away—the big halo lights up to signal the good news.

Hard to believe though it may be, the Angels' home is the fourth oldest big-league park, trailing only Fenway Park (1912), Wrigley Field (1914), and Dodger Stadium (1962). It is pretty amazing that one of its original features has not only endured but continues to serve as its defining characteristic.

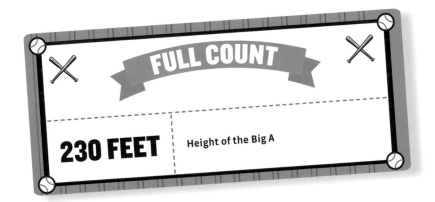

FULL COUNT

230 FEET Height of the Big A

The Big A towers over the
Angel Stadium parking lot
and Orange Freeway.

People ride the Giant Wheel in the early innings of an August 2015 game. The Wheel provides a colorful light show all game long on the left field berm.

THE GIANT WHEEL AT MODERN WOODMEN PARK

While many ballparks have play areas for kids these days, nowhere do you find a plaything as dramatic, massive, and beautiful as the 120-foot-tall Giant Wheel at Modern Woodmen Park. Situated atop the park's left field seating berm on the banks of the Mississippi River, the full-size Ferris wheel offers views of the field from nearly three times the height of the Green Monster Seats in Boston.

If you fork over five dollars to take a spin, not only can you peer down at a baseball diamond from a vantage point unlike any you have experienced before, but you can also survey the mansions of Davenport's "Gold Coast," Rock Island, and the majestic Centennial Bridge, which arches over the Mississippi on the park's right field side. As the wheel makes its 7.5-mile-per-hour rotation, you realize just how breezy it is so high aloft. You peer across the water into Illinois and look down at players who appear no larger than a child's toys.

Fans in the home plate stands also enjoy an amazing view thanks to the thousands of synchronized LED lights that trace the wheel's circumference and spokes. Together, the lights can produce more than a million different patterns that constantly change throughout the game. Imagine combining the enjoyment of watching a minor-league game with the pleasure of watching a laser light show!

The $1.05 million amusement park ride was built on location during the spring of 2014 after the River Bandits had installed smaller rides at their park in previous offseasons. In addition to taking a spin on game day, you can also stop by the park on non-game days throughout the summer to enjoy a bird's-eye view of Modern Woodmen Park.

 Ballpark Chatter

"There I sway, merely a slight sway, with the wind whispering around me. Only the sky is my partner. It is an ethereal feeling . . . At the tippity-top, the Ferris wheel stops. I am celestial. It is a feeling of never-ever having been so high in the sky."

—BILL WUNDRAM, COLUMNIST, WRITING IN THE *QUAD CITY TIMES*

22 *Cleveland Indians*

THE DRUMMER AT PROGRESSIVE FIELD

Who has played the most games at Progressive Field? That's an easy one. The same guy who played the most at Municipal Stadium: drumming John Adams!

Adams's strange journey to big-league stardom began on August 24, 1973, when the twenty-one-year-old Indians fan decided to haul a 26-inch bass drum to Municipal Stadium for a Friday night game between the Indians and Rangers. The Indians were on their way to a last place finish, and Adams figured they could use the extra encouragement his drum would offer.

The Indians won 11–5 that night, and a funny thing happened: A reporter from the *Cleveland Press* made his way out to the left field bleachers to interview Adams and wrote a story about him. As he read the article the next day, Adams decided to return to Municipal Stadium with his drum for the Saturday game. The Indians won that one too, and there was no doubt in Adams's mind he would be returning the next day. And the one after that . . .

More than four decades later, the Indians have long-since moved to a new park, and Adams's hair has grayed a bit, but if the Indians have a home game, you can pretty much bet your Cory Synder rookie cards that John Adams will be banging his drum. He has "played" more than 3,500 games, including all of the Indians postseason games in the 1990s and 2000s. The Indians have granted Adams two complimentary season tickets per year—one for him and one for his drum. You can spy Adams in Section 183, Row Y, in deep left-center field, but chances are you will hear him first!

FULL COUNT

3,500+ Games John Adams has spent with his drum in the Cleveland bleachers

Indians drummer John Adams, seen here beating his drum during a June 2016 game against the Royals

Fans can enjoy this Diamondbacks oasis beneath the Arizona sun.

THE SWIMMING POOL AT CHASE FIELD

As Maricopa County designed a home for the fledgling Arizona Diamondbacks in the 1990s, it sought to endow the park with a finishing touch that would signal to those in the stands or watching at home that theirs was a distinctly Arizonan park. While a rock and cactus garden might have served the purpose, the stadium's creators ambitiously chose to make another staple of the suburban Phoenix landscape the park's calling card—the backyard swimming pool.

When the Diamondbacks' park opened in 1998, it introduced a whole new kind of luxury viewing area to the baseball world: an 8,500-gallon swimming pool placed prominently atop the right field fence. There, some 415 feet from home plate, thirty-five fans per game swim, float, splash, and lounge while enjoying a view of the field.

Chances are you won't get to experience this ballpark oasis for yourself . . . unless you happen to have thirty-four friends who would like to visit Chase Field with you, toting their bathing suits, and chipping in about $200 each for the privilege of enjoying the pool, abutting hot tub, pool deck, locker room, and shower facilities beneath the stands. Nonetheless, your visit to Chase Field is sure to be enhanced by the pool's presence. Looking at the sparkling water, you can't help but chuckle at the bikini- and bathing-trunk-clad patrons partying in the outfield. And you watch the flight of long flyballs to right field with added interest, too, to see if they will make a splash.

Future Diamondback Mark Grace was the first player to knock a ball into the drink in the park's first season as a member of the visiting Chicago Cubs. Nearly fifty players have since followed suit, not including those who sent the horsehide into the chlorinated water when Chase Field hosted the All-Star Game and Home Run Derby in 2011.

" *Ballpark Chatter* "

"I could call it disrespectful and classless, but they don't have a beautiful pool at their old park and must have really wanted to see what one was like."

—JOHN MCCAIN, ARIZONA SENATOR, AFTER THE DODGERS CELEBRATED THEIR 2013 NL WEST TITLE BY TAKING A DIP IN THE CHASE FIELD POOL

24 *Chicago White Sox*

THE EXPLODING SCOREBOARD AT U.S. CELLULAR FIELD

In 1960 Bill Veeck unveiled a scoreboard like none the game had ever seen. Rising above Comiskey Park's center field fence, it measured 130 feet long and was loaded with gunpowder. Whenever a member of the White Sox hit a home run, it set the sky ablaze. Before long, Veeck refined the board further, installing on its ten launch tubes lightbulbs that lit in a sequence that made it look like they were spinning.

While Veeck's innovation was an immediate hit in Chicago, the other team owners said it was gaudy. Opposing pitchers said it showed them up. Cleveland outfielder Jimmy Piersall threw a baseball at it. The Yankees mocked it, parading on the field with sparklers after Clete Boyer and Mickey Mantle homered in Chicago. Even Veeck's wife, Mary Frances, said the board "wasn't very genteel." But Veeck knew—as he always did—what the fans wanted. And, let's face it: We Americans have always loved fireworks.

The White Sox' current home, U.S. Cellular Field, sports a later version of Veeck's Exploding Scoreboard that is even more spectacular than the original. Equipped with seven launchers and the same spinning wheels the fans on Chicago's South Side have loved for generations, it turns every White Sox homer into a visual feast.

According to an interview Veeck's son Mike gave to the *New York Times* after Veeck's death, the senior Veeck dreamt up the board while watching the William Saroyan play *The Time of Your Life*. The story is set at a San Francisco bar where one of the characters beats the house pinball machine, which reflects his elation by making all kinds of joyous noises and flashes.

U.S. CELLULAR FIELD

- Run the **Comiskey Park bases** in the U.S. Cellular Field parking lot

- Visit **Champions Plaza**, which celebrates the 2005 World Series winners with a multi-player sculpture

- Find the **two blue seats** in the outfield stands marking the landing spots of key Paul Konerko and Scott Podsednik homers during the 2005 World Series

BALLPARK BUCKET LIST

The White Sox's famous Exploding Scoreboard

Nostalgia Man towers over the
AutoZone Park entrance gates.

THE NOSTALGIA MAN STATUE AT AUTOZONE PARK

After the Memphis Chicks announced at the end of the 1997 season that they would be leaving for Jackson, Tennessee, Memphis was granted membership into the Pacific Coast League. The new club would be permitted to play at aging Tim McCarver Stadium until it built a new yard. With a temporary ballpark and player development contract with the St. Louis Cardinals, the fledgling team was on its way, but it still needed to come up with a name for itself, a logo, and a staff. As a placeholder, team founder Dean Jernigan began using an old-time player silhouette atop team letterhead. The logo portrayed a lefty-swinger in a white uniform leaning forward to take what could only be a mighty cut. Set against the backdrop of a black oval, the image was simple and clean. The local fans fell in love with it.

Dubbed "Nostalgia Man," the image was adopted as the team's official logo by the time the Memphis Redbirds took the field at beautiful AutoZone Park in 2000, and it was the impetus for a 40-foot-tall statue at the park's main entrance.

You can find the giant Nostalgia Man at the corner of Union Avenue and South 3rd Street, guarding against any rogue Grizzlies or River Cats that might try to infiltrate the home of their league rival. As far as minor-league entrances go, this is one of the most elaborate you will encounter . . . and one of the most delightful. Nostalgia Man tapped into a deep vein in the popular psyche when he was first introduced. The classic image of an anonymous player in simple gear playing the game we fans love stirred something in our hearts. That romantic notion—that nostalgia—is worth something to us. And it is personified wonderfully in Memphis.

> ❝ *Ballpark Chatter* ❞
>
> **Nostalgia (noun)—Pleasure and sadness that is caused by remembering something from the past and wishing that you could experience it again**
>
> —*MERRIAM-WEBSTER* DEFINITION OF NOSTALGIA

26 *Detroit Tigers*

THE OUTFIELD STATUES AT COMERICA PARK

Above Comerica Park's redbrick wall in deep left field, you find a row of large metallic sculptures honoring six Tigers greats: Charlie Gehringer, Hank Greenberg, Ty Cobb, Willie Horton, Al Kaline, and Hal Newhouser. Since the park's opening in 2000, these handsome steel statues have reminded fans of these legends' grace and prowess while synthesizing the Tigers' proud past with their present.

A notorious hard-slider, Cobb is depicted with his spikes flying high as he swipes a base. Newhouser is captured in the midst of an even higher leg-kick as he rears back to deliver a pitch. Gehringer is air-borne after making a throw to first base to complete a double play. Greenberg is frozen in mid-swing in the moment after bat collides with ball. Kaline leaps to make a game-saving catch, his glove extended above an imaginary right field fence. Horton finishes a prodigious cut, as the air ripples behind his bat.

Each statue's pedestal displays biographical information and statistics. Gehringer's write-up describes him as "a quiet man, who played with remarkable grace and efficiency." Cobb's describes him as "perhaps the greatest player in baseball history."

After entering the park, you can follow the concourse to the outfield area and inspect the statues up-close. Then, you can head to your seat and enjoy them all game long from a different vantage point. Printed beneath each statue on the brick wall facing the field are the last name and retired uniform number of each statue's subject. On the right field Wall of Fame, meanwhile, you find the names of other Tigers stars like Mickey Cochrane, George Kell, Harry Heilmann, Sam Crawford, Heinie Manush, and Hughie Jennings. Jackie Robinson and longtime Tigers manager Sparky Anderson are also honored here, as is late Tigers broadcaster Ernie Harwell.

COMERICA PARK

- Visit the **Willie Horton Field of Dreams** (2121 Trumbull Avenue), a youth field on the former Tiger Stadium site

- Peruse decades' worth of memorabilia at **Nemo's** (1384 Michigan Avenue), the classic watering hole for Tigers fans

- Take a spin on the **Fly Ball Ferris Wheel** at Comerica Park's food court

BALLPARK BUCKET LIST

23
ORTON

COBB

5
GREENBERG

2
GEHRINGER

16
NEWHOUSER

6
KALINE

The Tigers greats—including Ty Cobb stealing a base—are captured in steel beyond the left field fence.

The red seat

THE RED SEAT AT FENWAY PARK

Come game-time, Fenway Park's outfield bleachers present a roiling sea of red and blue shirts and hats. But when the old park's gates first open, you find an entirely different hue filling—or nearly filling—the bleachers: a sea of green that is interrupted only by the lone red seat two-thirds of the way up the stands, high above the visitors' bullpen.

Known as "The Red Seat" or "The Ted Williams Seat," this simple plastic chair is as popular a pre-game destination for Fenway pilgrims as the left field corner where you can reach out and knock your knuckles against the Green Monster. The seat marks the landing spot of a prodigious 502-foot home run struck by Williams in 1946. No Fenway homer has come close to reaching it since, not even the ones blasted by Mark McGwire, Sammy Sosa, and the other over-inflated sluggers of the era when they visited Fenway for the 1999 Home Run Derby.

The seat is in Section 42, Row 37, and labeled Seat 21, even though seats didn't exist in the bleachers when Williams launched a changeup from Detroit's Fred Hutchinson into orbit one fine June afternoon. Wooden benches filled Fenway's bleachers then, and sitting upon one of those slabs of wood was a construction engineer from Albany, New York, named Joseph Boucher.

Boucher was wearing a straw hat . . . a straw hat he would carry from Fenway in tatters after Williams's homer landed on his head. In compensation, Red Sox owner Tom Yawkey awarded Boucher a lifetime pass to Fenway Park.

The Red Sox replaced the bleacher benches with seats in the 1970s, and then reseated the area again in 1984. Red Sox executive Haywood Sullivan then had the idea to install the one red seat to show fans how far Williams' shot traveled. And red it has remained ever since.

FENWAY PARK

- Snap a photo of the **Ted Williams Jimmy Fund statue** outside Fenway Park's Gate B

- Shag batting practice homers behind the **right field bullpens**, which were dubbed Williamsburg when the Red Sox brought in the right field fence to create a shorter porch for "The Kid" in 1940

- Find **Williams's retired No. 9** on the right field façade

BALLPARK BUCKET LIST

Blast from the Past!

★ **THE ROCKFORD PEACHES** ★
THE ALL-AMERICAN GIRLS PROFESSIONAL BASEBALL LEAGUE, 1943–1954

As many major and minor leaguers headed to foreign theaters during the war years, the All-American Girls Professional Baseball League (AAGPBL) filled the entertainment void on the homefront. At its height, the league attracted nearly a million fans in 1948. The Peaches, of Rockford, Illinois, were the circuit's most successful team, winning titles in 1945, 1948, 1949, and 1950.

THE PEACHES AND THE FIRST WOMAN TO PITCH TO THE BOYS

- The Rockford Peaches played at Beyer Stadium, the original ticket booth of which still stands in Rockford today.
- The Peaches were one of two teams to play in all twelve of the AAGPBL's seasons, the other being the Blue Sox of South Bend, Indiana.
- Ila Borders became the first woman to play professional baseball with men, pitching fifteen games for the St. Paul Saints in 1997.

THE DESERT SETTING AT CAMELBACK RANCH–GLENDALE

Camelback Ranch–Glendale presents a version of the American ballpark infused by the stark landscape and earthy tones of the Sonoran Desert. With a design that is spacious, clean, and elegant, the park offers its own unique take on the concept of the baseball pastoral.

Before you even reach the ballpark gates, you begin to appreciate its originality. You follow a desert path through a rocky landscape that features a small oasis, desert plants, rock walls, stone veneers, and twelve practice fields. Stone buildings along the way reflect the colors and irregular angles of the mountain peaks that ring the Salt River Valley.

At last, you reach a structure that looks more like a hunter's lodge than a stadium, especially inside, where a slatted sunroof shields the home plate grandstand from rays that only grow stronger as March progresses. Home plate's southeast orientation also allows for a bit more shade than you find at most Cactus League parks, which face northeast. As a bonus, the orientation shows off the peaks of the South Mountains beyond the right field fence.

The brown and caramel color scheme of the concrete, the rust-colored metal, and slanting angles of the stadium all contribute further to its stark desert feel, as do the gabion walls lining the concourses with desert stones held in place by metal framing. The see-through scoreboard is also unique. Located atop the right field berm, it consists of scaffolding connecting a face-clock with a video board with a line score. Usually ballpark designers just put advertising in the spaces on the scoreboard that don't provide game information, but at Camelback Ranch you find a board through which you can look upon the desert landscape that inspired so many other aspects of the park.

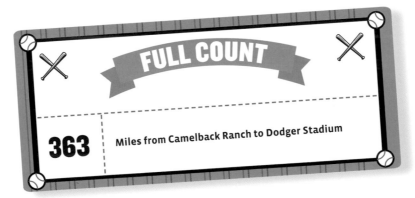

FULL COUNT

363 | Miles from Camelback Ranch to Dodger Stadium

Caramel seats and rustic
grandstand, the South
Mountains rising on the right
field horizon, and a see-through
scoreboard

The right field diehards
cheer on their A's.

THE BLEACHER DIEHARDS AT OAKLAND COLISEUM

The Oakland A's boast some of the most rabid fans in all of baseball . . . not a whole stadium full of them . . . but a few sections' worth in the first rows of the left and right field bleachers. Game after game, the green-and-gold-clad diehards turn out, toting banners, drums, tambourines, cowbells, and other instruments. The locus of the troupe is Section 149 in right field. There, above the out-of-town scoreboard, the most zealous rooters rib visiting right fielders, raise their fingers in unison after each defensive out, and sing, "We love you Oakland, we do / We love you Oakland, we do / Oooak-land we love you!" whenever an Oakland runner crosses the plate. They also chant, "Baaaaall four, baaaaall four, baaaaall four," and wave four fingers toward the plate whenever an A's hitter runs up a three-ball count.

This multi-generational FANily first gained national prominence in 2001 after the A's featured them in a series of television commercials and promised them free tickets to any home playoff games. When the A's hosted the Yankees for Games Three and Four of the American League Division Series, the team made good on its promise, only to see Yankees owner George Steinbrenner complain to the league office, citing an obscure rule limiting noise made by fans receiving complimentary tickets.

In truth, the A's bleacher brigade is pretty friendly, especially to visiting players who have a sense of humor. Most famously, they once developed a friendship with visiting right fielder Jeff Francoeur, who one day tossed a ball to them with a $100 bill taped to it and a note to spend it on bacon and beer. Another time, they tossed a Butterfinger at Josh Hamilton to thank him for muffing a catch that helped the A's win the American League West title in 2012.

OAKLAND COLISEUM

- Enjoy the low-tech **dot-race** on the scoreboard between innings

- Order a **"Big Atomic Hot" beef and pork sausage** from the Saag's stand behind Section 118

- Bop along to the Phenomenauts' **"Theme for Oakland"** when the A's win

BALLPARK BUCKET LIST

30 *Brooklyn Cyclones*
THE NEON SKYLINE AT MCU PARK

The Brooklyn Cyclones' festive Coney Island home, MCU Park, does a great job of capturing the beach and boardwalk spirit of its surroundings.

After traversing a ballpark concourse illuminated by colorful neon tracers that may have you wondering if you've taken a wrong turn and stumbled into the labyrinth of carnival rides outside the park, you feel the sea breeze on your face as you step into a grandstand that directs your gaze at the famous Coney Island rides beyond the outfield fence.

A corkscrewing roller coaster, known as the Thunderbolt, twists and turns behind the left field wall, while the iconic Coney Island Cyclone scares the bejesus out of the brave souls who zip along its wooden tracks. The 150-foot-tall Wonder Wheel spins slowly in the distance.

In right field, you find the Parachute Jump. Constructed for the 1939 World's Fair, the 250-foot-tall structure has been called the Eiffel Tower of Brooklyn. With its slender trunk and wide top, it looks like a mechanical palm tree, especially when illuminated in hot pink and other colors at night. Back in its heyday, the ride would hoist people to its top and then drop them, letting their parachutes deliver them to the ground.

MCU Park's left field scoreboard is adorned with a miniature roller coaster, which mimics the rise and fall of the real tracks just behind it. The coaster even offers cutouts of little riders, who throw their hands in the air in jubilation as the car descends.

The ballpark light banks reflect the local vibe too, thanks to the colorful neon ring that encircles each one with a purple, pink, green, red, or rainbow halo.

Together, these glowing rides and ballpark features create a kaleidoscope that couldn't exist anywhere else but Coney Island.

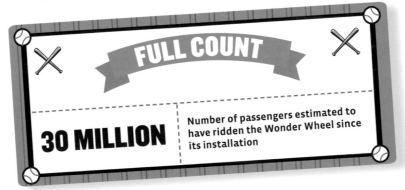

FULL COUNT

30 MILLION — Number of passengers estimated to have ridden the Wonder Wheel since its installation

MCU Park's roller coaster scoreboard and neon-ringed light towers fit the Coney Island landscape perfectly, and the Parachute Jump—which lights up at night—dwarfs the right field pole and light towers.

The Liberty Bell replica lights up at night.

THE LIBERTY BELL AT CITIZENS BANK PARK

On May 16, 1972, twenty-one-year-old Greg Luzinski stepped to the plate at Philadelphia's Veterans Stadium and connected with a fastball served up by Chicago Cubs righty Burt Hooton. As the crack of the bat echoed throughout the cavernous stadium, the ball sailed directly over the pitcher's mound, seemingly gaining speed as it rose higher and higher above the infield, outfield, outfield fence, and then three levels of seating. Finally, the ball clanked down on the 400 level, dinging Veterans Stadium's famous Liberty Bell replica some 500 feet from home plate.

In the Vet's thirty-three seasons hosting big-league ball, no other slugger came close to ringing the Liberty Bell. Still, the replica of Philadelphia's symbol of American Independence was a beloved ballpark fixture, and when the Phillies opened their new park in 2004, they wisely chose to recreate it at Citizens Bank Park. You find the new bell mounted on metal scaffolding high above the right-center field fence. It is more than just an ornament; it is a home-run celebration machine, as well.

The 50-foot-high, 35-foot-wide bell and clapper are outlined in multicolored neon lights that glow in a pattern that makes it look like the bell is swinging from side to side whenever a member of the Phillies connects for a long ball. The stars on the bell light up too, and a loud gong reverberates as the conquering player circles the bases.

You will notice that the Phillies' bell even includes a neon representation of the vertical crack that first appeared on the real Liberty Bell in the early 1800s. You can pay homage to that national treasure at Philadelphia's Independence National Historic Park while you are in town.

CITIZENS BANK PARK

- Raise your hands in triumph beside the famous **Rocky Balboa statue** outside the Philadelphia Museum of Art (2600 Benjamin Franklin Parkway)
- Visit the **Liberty Bell** at Independence National Park (41 N. 6th Street)
- Stroll down **Memory Lane**, an illustrated history of Philadelphia baseball, behind the Citizens Bank Park batter's eye

BALLPARK BUCKET LIST

32 *Seattle Mariners*
THE ROOF AT SAFECO FIELD

Come rain or shine, you are guaranteed an outdoor baseball game when you visit Seattle's Safeco Field, all thanks to the game's most innovative roof. Since its debut in 1999, the Mariners' ballpark lid has left room for fresh air to waft across the field and stands even when it is "closed." That's because unlike the roofs in Phoenix and Houston, where heat-relief is the objective, Safeco's roof exists to serve as a giant umbrella. It takes the form of three independent sections that stack up neatly over the BNSF Railway tracks in Safeco's right field corner when the weather is clear. When storm clouds gather, it literally rolls out on steel wheels affixed to tall trusses that run along elevated tracks. There are three parallel tracks, one for each of the telescoping panels.

Another virtue of the roof is its height. It hovers 215 feet above the field as it covers 9 acres of field and stands. By comparison, the roof at Tropicana Field is only 85 feet above the playing surface at points across the outfield. Safeco's roof is so high that it covers the right-center field scoreboard and the out-field light towers with room to spare.

It takes about ten minutes for the roof to open or close, and if you are lucky you might see it retract or roll out during your visit to Safeco. Usually, the Mariners make a decision on whether it should be opened or closed prior to the game and it remains in one position for the full nine, but if a storm crops up earlier than expected or a rainy day turns into a sunny one, the M's can roll it out or roll it back as needed. So, leave your poncho and galoshes at home when you visit Safeco Field; you won't need them!

" *Ballpark Chatter* "

"I guess things like this happen. Sometimes your garbage disposal doesn't work. Sometimes your washing machine doesn't work. Sometimes your personal computer doesn't work."
—CHUCK ARMSTRONG, FORMER MARINERS PRESIDENT, AFTER A ROOF MALFUNCTION CAUSED A FIFTY-FOUR-MINUTE RAIN DELAY IN JULY 2000

The roof sits stacked on the right side of the park.

The cotton presses
that flank the
Whataburger Field
scoreboard date
back to the 1920s.

THE COTTON PRESSES AT WHATABURGER FIELD

The two large cotton presses incorporated into Whataburger Field's outfield design highlight Corpus Christi's proud cotton-producing heritage. In the heart of the old cotton district, the presses stand where they have since the early 1920s, although they no longer serve their prior purpose of compressing loose cotton into tidy bails suitable for transport. Today, they stand in left field home-run territory, flanking one of the largest video boards in the Texas League and providing the home of the Corpus Christi Hooks with a nostalgic finishing touch.

Wisely, the Hooks made the decision to only partially restore them. Their corrugated steel siding bears a fair amount of rust and several of their windows are missing or broken. The weathered look lends them authenticity. They are no mere props. They were here first. And while they may be relics from an era that has passed, they are still standing.

While it takes a pretty good poke for a hitter to reach the presses, they have been assailed by flyballs on occasion. Corpus Christi fans still talk about the time future big leaguer Hunter Pence reached the press nearest the left field foul line with a batting practice homer in 2006. That season, Pence slugged 28 long balls for the Hooks, but the one everyone still remembers didn't show up on the stat sheet. Pence hit a towering shot to left during his cage session that shattered one of the windows, and to commemorate it, the Hooks added a sign on the press that reads simply BAM-BAM, which was Pence's nickname during his time in Corpus Christi. Chances are you won't see a window-smashing shot when you visit Whataburger Field, but here's betting you enjoy a game played in the shadows of these unique ballpark landmarks.

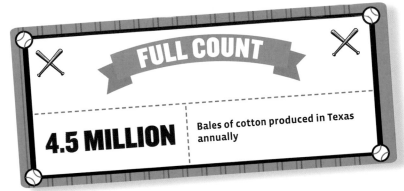

FULL COUNT

4.5 MILLION | Bales of cotton produced in Texas annually

34 *St. Louis Cardinals*
THE GATEWAY ARCH AT BUSCH STADIUM

For years, the synthesis between the Gateway City's defining characteristic and its proud baseball tradition was practically nonexistent as the Cardinals played within the enclosed Busch Memorial Stadium. In the old Busch Stadium, only those seated along the first base side could spy the top of the Gateway Arch peaking over the left side of the stadium. But all that changed in 2006 when the team swung open the gates to new Busch Stadium, which showcases the Arch rising majestically across its outfield view. As the sun sets on the manmade marvel, it is truly a sight to behold. Today, anyone sitting around the infield or along the baselines enjoys a view of the Arch in all its glory.

Built as a monument to Thomas Jefferson's notion of St. Louis as the gateway to the western expansion of the United States, the Arch took two and a half years to build. It was meant to provide St. Louis with a recognizable emblem and world-class tourist attraction and in both regards succeeded. Interestingly, its legs stand 630 feet apart, matching its height. At ground level, the base of each leg measures 54 feet across; at the apex, 63 stories above the ground, the arch measures just 17 feet across.

In recent years, the Busch Stadium grounds crew has gotten into the spirit too, often mowing a massive Arch pattern into the outfield grass. The feet of the lawn arch can be found behind the first and third base bags, while the apex crests in deep center. When the grass is freshly cut, it is impossible to miss this delightful finishing touch, whether you're watching the game in person or on TV.

" *Ballpark Chatter* "

"Let us hope that the Arch . . . becomes, far in the future, a mysterious structure like the Great Pyramids . . . that leads onlookers to wonder about the people who produced it and ask themselves what strange compulsions led to its creation."

—TRACY CAMPBELL, *THE GATEWAY ARCH: A BIOGRAPHY*

The Gateway Arch and the arch mowed into the Busch Stadium lawn

Fans enjoy Frisco's
Choctaw Lazy River.

THE LAZY RIVER AT DR PEPPER BALLPARK

Shaped something like a giant figure-eight, the Choctaw Lazy River takes you on a 400-foot ride across the Dr Pepper Ballpark outfield and back . . . a distance roughly equivalent to how far a batted ball must travel to splash down in its 3-foot-deep waters. The two center-circles of the figure-eight serve as islands upon which you can sit and watch the game. Two cabanas line the riverbank, making sure you are well stocked with food and drink.

To put in perspective just how revolutionary this moving body of water is, consider that the 68,000-gallon circulating pool holds eight times more water than the seminal baseball oasis at Chase Field in Arizona. According to the RoughRiders, it would take about a million cups of nacho cheese to fill the Lazy River.

The perennial Texas League attendance leaders announced their intent to build the $1.5 million lagoon in February 2016, and by June it had opened. Best of all, it offers regular fans a chance to get wet too. While it *is* reserved for private groups on most dates, on Thursdays you can purchase a river pass and enjoy a full nine innings of luxury splash-viewing. For $39, you enjoy river access, a flotation device, a pregame music show, and all-you-can-eat hot dogs, brats, chips, peanuts, and soda.

Even sitting in the stands, your enjoyment of a game in Frisco is enhanced by the view of the river, the 113-foot-long waterfall atop the outfield fence, and the two 18-foot-high projection walls behind the river that create a visually-pleasing effect that is half fountain and half laser light show.

For making a splash with an original idea, the RoughRiders deserve a tip of the cap and flip of the swim fins!

FULL COUNT

1.2 MILLION   Baseballs it would take to fill the RoughRiders' lazy river

THE SCOREBOARD AT WRIGLEY FIELD

Atop Wrigley Field's pyramid-shaped bleachers, you find baseball's most charming scoreboard. The hand-operated tally board stands as a relic of the ballpark experience of yesteryear. Yes, two new video boards flank it now, but the old three-story board rises considerably higher than them, ensuring it is still the park's most prominent outfield structure. Since its installation in 1937, it has retained all its other essential characteristics too.

Three Cubs employees operate the board after climbing a ladder atop the bleachers to access its trap door. They insert steel numeral plates into its face to update the Cubs line score and the line scores of up to eleven other games being played across the major leagues. Because there were just sixteen teams when the board was built, it does not offer room for every big-league game on its face. Usually the West Coast games get left off.

The board offers the NL line scores in the left column, with the Cubs game always at the bottom, and the AL scores in the right column. Unlike any other scoreboard, it stops short of tallying the runs from games in progress in a total runs scored column, meaning you need to do actual math to compute each game's score, adding up the inning totals.

More practically, the board shows the balls, strikes, and outs of the game being played on the Wrigley lawn thanks to another scoreboard operator who sits in the press box above home plate.

As for the flagpole atop the scoreboard, it hangs the pennants of all fifteen National League teams from its crossbar in the order of each team's place in the standings. And after each Cubs win, the scoreboard operators hoist a large white flag bearing a blue W to signal to folks outside the park that the Cubs have been victorious.

WRIGLEY FIELD

- Visit the original **Billy Goat Tavern** (430 N. Michigan Ave.), where the legend of the Cubs' curse first took root after owner Bill Sianis was told he couldn't bring his pet goat Murphy to Game Four of the 1945 World Series
- Shag batting practice homers **behind the left field bleachers**
- Peruse the **statues of former Cubs** on the streets surrounding the park, including likenesses of Ernie Banks, Billy Williams, Ron Santo, and beloved announcer Harry Caray

BALLPARK BUCKET LIST

The Wrigley Field scoreboard with its colorful pennants of every National League team has risen over the center field bleachers since 1937.

TARGET FIELD

Minnie and Paul light up the night and shake hands over the Mississippi River.

THE MINNIE AND PAUL SIGN AT TARGET FIELD

The most prominent of Target Field's many delightful finishing touches is the gigantic, animated rendering of the Twins logo high above the center field batter's eye. The "Minnie and Paul" sign, as it is known, depicts two big-bellied ballplayers—one wearing an M on his jersey and the other wearing the initials S, T, P. The two gents shake hands over the Mississippi River, which forms the natural border between the Twin Cities of Minneapolis and St. Paul.

The creative logo was sketched in 1961 by a freelance illustrator from St. Paul named Ray Barton, who was under the impression the logo would merely be used on Metropolitan Stadium cups and napkins during the Twins' inaugural season after they relocated from Washington, DC, where they had played as the Senators. He had no idea that his sketch would become the team's official insignia or that half a century later it would be animated in neon over the Twins' third Minnesota home.

The sign launches into different celebration modes in response to game developments. When a Twins player hits a home run, for example, Minnie and Paul light up and shake hands over the flowing river. When the Twins score a run by other means, the lights bordering the sign create a strobe effect to simulate a player rounding the bases. When a Twins pitcher records a strikeout, the corners of the sign light up to replicate the borders of the strike zone. And when the Twins lock up a victory, the T and the S in Twins flash on and off to spell TWINS WIN.

This is the best kind of ballpark celebration machine, one that offers a nod to the home team's identity while being just cheesy enough to be utterly endearing.

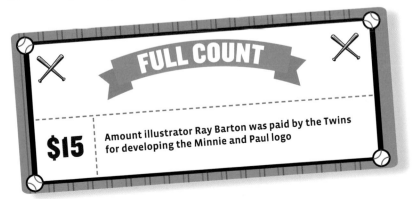

FULL COUNT

$15 Amount illustrator Ray Barton was paid by the Twins for developing the Minnie and Paul logo

38 *Colorado Rockies*

THE MILE HIGH SEATS AT COORS FIELD

Coors Field is widely considered the most hitter-friendly park in baseball. In the Rocky Mountain air, breaking balls flatten out, becoming more hittable, and high flyballs tend to keep on flying until they touch down somewhere in home-run territory. The Rockies' diamond lies almost a mile above sea level, amid air considerably thinner and dryer than what we breathe in other big-league cities. Just how altitudinous is Coors Field compared to the game's other yards? Well, at 5,259 feet above sea level, it is nearly five times loftier than the second highest park—Arizona's Chase field (1,082 feet), and only six other big-league teams play at parks that exceed 600 feet above sea level.

To celebrate the environmental phenomenon that makes the games played on its field unique, Coors Field features a single row of purple seats in its upper deck denoting the exact point where the elevation reaches 5,280 feet, or, 1 mile above sea level. When the deck is nearly full, you can scarcely notice this ballpark novelty, but when Coors Field first opens its gates the row of purple really stands out against the forest green seats that otherwise fill the stands. If you hold a ticket to any seat in Row 20, you find your bottom perched exactly a mile above the Pacific Ocean; if you sit in Rows 21–26, you are *more than* a mile above the nearest waves.

Even if you are sitting on one of the lower levels, you may want to head upstairs to snap the ultimate Coors Field photo, reclined a mile above sea level in a purple chair. As an added attraction, the third deck offers the park's best views of the snowcapped Rockies, which rise in the distance beyond the left and center field fences.

" *Ballpark Chatter* "

"Is Coors Field a good park to hit in? Yeah. So are Wrigley Field and Camden Yards. I didn't design Coors Field—I just play there."

—TODD HELTON, FORMER ROCKIES STAR

The purple seats that ring the entire upper deck at Coors Field are exactly 1 mile above sea level.

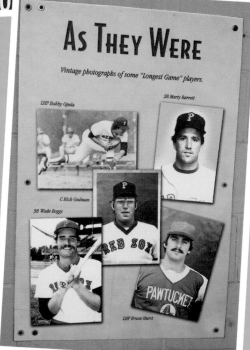

THE LONGEST GAME EXHIBIT AT MCCOY STADIUM

Pawtucket's charming World War II era stadium offers a tribute to the longest professional baseball game ever played: a thirty-three-inning marathon between the Pawtucket Red Sox and Rochester Red Wings on April 18, 1981.

Despite frigid temperatures, 1,740 fans turned out. The first nine progressed swiftly enough, as Red Wings starter Larry Jones carried a 1–0 shutout into the final frame. But the PawSox scored on a wild pitch to send the game into extras. More than two hours later, the Red Wings regained the lead in the top of the twenty-first; in the bottom of the inning, though, Wade Boggs tied the score with an RBI double.

The International League had a curfew rule that said no inning could begin after 12:50 a.m., but it had been accidentally omitted from the league handbook that year, and home plate umpire Dennis Cregg ruled the game should continue. And continue it did, until 4:07 a.m. when Pawtucket general manager Mike Tamburro finally woke up International League president Harold Cooper with a phone call. Cooper said the teams should suspend play. And so, after thirty-two innings, the nineteen fans remaining in the stands headed home.

When the game resumed on a warm June afternoon, a sellout crowd of 5,746 people jammed McCoy Stadium to witness the spectacle. The game that had seemed impossible to end in the chill of April yielded quickly to its place in the history books beneath the June sun, ending after eighteen minutes when Pawtucket's Dave Koza stroked a single in the bottom of the thirty third to plate Marty Barrett and deliver a 3–2 win. In all, the game took eight hours and twenty-five minutes.

The exhibit at McCoy provides vintage photos, period newspaper articles about the game, a list of the many records the game set, and the home plate from the game.

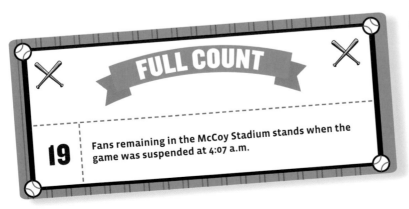

FULL COUNT

19 Fans remaining in the McCoy Stadium stands when the game was suspended at 4:07 a.m.

★ THE LIGHTS AT CROSLEY FIELD, ★ CINCINNATI REDS, MAY 24, 1935

As big-league teams struggled to draw fans during the Great Depression, Cincinnati Reds general manager Larry MacPhail convinced team owner Powell Crosley to spend $50,000 on a lighting system for Crosley Field. After eight towers were erected, the Reds hosted the Phillies for Major League Baseball's first night game. President Franklin Delano Roosevelt threw the ceremonial "first switch" at the White House before the Reds downed the Phillies 2–1. Pictured here, Philadelphia's Ethan Allen awaits a pitch from Paul Derringer.

A LIGHT HISTORY OF BASEBALL

- The major leagues were late to the night baseball party. Some sixty-five minor-league teams had already installed lights at their fields by the start of the 1935 season.

- The 1935 Reds went on to finish with a 68-85 record but drew more than twice as many fans as they had the year before, thanks to the popularity of Crosley Field's eight night games.

- Brooklyn's Ebbets Field became the second major-league facility to host night baseball on June 15, 1938, as Cincinnati's Johnny Vander Meer pitched his second consecutive no-hitter against the Dodgers.

40 *Toronto Blue Jays*
THE HOTEL ROOMS AT ROGERS CENTRE

Upon opening in 1989, Toronto's SkyDome was hailed as an engineering marvel. Its thirty-one-story-high retractable roof meant the Blue Jays and their opponents could play outdoor baseball on nice days and indoor baseball on rainy or snowy ones. The stadium also brought the game its first-ever built-in ballpark hotel. Booking one of the Renaissance Downtown Toronto's seventy field-facing rooms allows you to watch a game from the comfort of what equates to your own private luxury box.

As a traveling fan, your best option is to book two or three nights at the Renaissance during a Blue Jays homestand. You can watch a game or two from the ballpark seats, sampling the stadium cuisine, and then watch a bonus game from your hotel room at no extra cost, enjoying the private bathroom, minibar, room service, and fridge.

In this land where the home team once played at a park named Exhibition Stadium, just be sure to close the drapes if you are planning to watch the game in your underwear. When they built the hotel, they opted to use two-way glass on its windows, thinking television viewers in far-away cities would see folks enjoying games from their rooms and would want to travel to Toronto to have the same experience themselves. As a result, on several occasions hotel guests have been spotted sans clothes or engaging in explicit demonstrations of their ... umm ... affection for each other. Hotel management took to stationing an employee in the stands with a pair of binoculars to monitor the field-facing windows. At the first sign of risqué behavior, the lookout notifies the front desk, which dispatches a hotel employee to the room to implore the occupants to close the drapes or at least move away from the window.

" *Ballpark Chatter* "

"We have a unique product here. Obviously, in hotel rooms around the world, who knows what happens. But here, it's kind of like a fishbowl."
—DAN WOODBURN, GENERAL MANAGER, RENAISSANCE DOWNTOWN TORONTO HOTEL

The hotel rooms above and beside the Rogers Centre video board offer a unique view of the field.

The B&O Warehouse, which measures 1,016 feet long from end to end, dominates the view on the right side of Oriole Park.

THE B&O WAREHOUSE AT ORIOLE PARK AT CAMDEN YARDS

In 1898 as three-year-old George Herman Ruth was toddling around his father's cafe on Baltimore's West Camden Street, construction began on a new railroad storage facility at Camden Station. Once completed, the 51-foot-wide, 1,016-foot-long B&O Warehouse climbed eight stories and stretched fully four blocks along South Eutaw Street. Who could have guessed that it would one day play a role in transforming the ballparks of America's Game . . . a sport the similarly revolutionary Ruth would soon begin playing?

Long after falling into disrepair in the 1970s, the longest freestanding building on the East Coast was fully restored in the early 1990s to complement the classic design of Oriole Park. In so channeling the spirit of the game's glorious past, the Orioles and their vintage warehouse started a national trend. Soon every city wanted a retro-classic park.

It cost more than $20 million to save the B&O, but it was worth it. Nearly all of the building's 900 windows had to be replaced—including sixty-three on the first and second floors that were outfitted with shatter-proof glass. The building's brick face had to be hand-cleaned to prevent mortar loss. And the interior had to be gutted and rebuilt. But by the time Oriole Park opened in 1992, the warehouse was ready to provide Oriole Park with its defining characteristic.

Even before you get to your seat, the B&O plays a role in the ballpark experience. After passing through the gates, you trace the building's path along Eutaw Street en route to the concourse, finding shops, restaurants, and even a statue of Ruth along the way.

Although the towering structure stands just 439 feet from home plate at its closest point, only one batted ball has reached it since Oriole Park's opening—a blast by Ken Griffey Jr. during the 1993 Home Run Derby.

ORIOLE PARK AT CAMDEN YARDS

- Visit the **Babe Ruth Birthplace and Museum** (216 Emory Street), where the Bambino was born
- Peruse the eighty-five (and counting) **bronze ball markers** on Eutaw Street, marking the landing spots of Oriole Park's longest home runs
- Inspect the **"Babe's Dream" statue** on South Eutaw Street and observe that Ruth is incorrectly depicted holding a right-handed fielder's glove

BALLPARK BUCKET LIST

42 *Portland Sea Dogs*
THE LIGHTHOUSE AT HADLOCK FIELD

At a ballpark that does a wonderful job of incorporating various elements of the Maine seacoast into its game-day presentation, the elusive 16-foot-tall retractable lighthouse that sits hidden behind the center field fence on a hydraulic lift is the highlight. Settling into your ballpark seat and snacking on a Sea Dog Biscuit or fried fish sandwich, you can see the seagulls circling overhead, and smell the salty ocean air, but Hadlock Field's magical lighthouse eludes you and will continue to until a member of the Sea Dogs hits a home run or until the team finishes off a win. Those are the only occasions that bring the lighthouse into sight.

When summoned, it rises from behind the 400-foot marker in center field amid a spray of Roman candle eruptions, while flash bulbs flicker throughout the park and young fans cry with glee. Upon reaching its apex, its bright white light spins around and around, while a foghorn drones. Then, having served its purpose, it retracts behind the fence once more.

This unique ballpark fixture has been a part of the Hadlock Field experience since the yard's opening in 1994. Team owner Dan Burke wanted to incorporate a lighthouse into the ballpark's design but didn't quite know how. Unbeknownst to him, John Rague, program and administrative services manager for the Portland Public Works Department, came up with the idea for a retractable lighthouse and hired a local carpenter to build it in the weeks leading up to the Sea Dogs' inaugural game. Amazingly, it was built and installed without Burke's knowledge. When the Sea Dogs hit their first ever Hadlock Field home run, a smile rose to their owner's face as he and the rest of the team's fans realized their yard had a very special celebration machine.

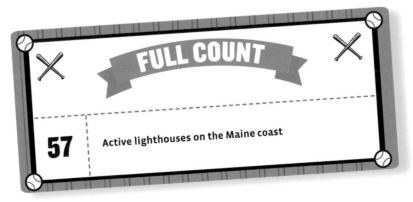

FULL COUNT

57 Active lighthouses on the Maine coast

The lighthouse, accompanied by flaring Roman candles, rises to celebrate a Sea Dogs home run.

The Royals crown-topped scoreboard reaches as high as the Kauffman Stadium light towers, and the back side celebrates the team's 2015 World Series victory.

THE CROWN SCOREBOARD AT KAUFFMAN STADIUM

There is no more ornate or apropos scoreboard in the big leagues than the ten-story-high wonder at Kauffman Stadium. The unique board is shaped like the Royals' crest and capped by a sparkling golden crown. An original ballpark feature that dates to Kauffman Stadium's opening in 1973, the Royals scoreboard celebrates the home team's identity while lending a further touch of class to a ballpark already teeming with it. The crown shimmers in the midday sun and beneath the ballpark lights, reminding you upon your every glance toward center field that you aren't sitting at any ballpark, but at a ballpark fit for a king . . . or queen.

The golden crown caps an 84-foot-wide, 104-foot-tall LED board that is one of the largest and most technologically sophisticated in the big leagues. As had been the case with the slightly smaller low-definition board that had stood in center field until 2009, today's version has a home-plate-shaped bottom.

Today's crown is more sparkly and three-dimensional than the one atop the old scoreboard was. Produced by a Kansas City metal fabrication company, it consists of stainless steel coated with shiny, iridescent flashing that doesn't take the form of a flat, continuous surface but of a compilation of different strips that causes light to reflect off each piece a little differently. As the sun or ballpark lights catch each piece of metal at a slightly different angle, the variance in reflection creates the sparkling effect. What's more, the four golden balls that adorn the peaks of the crown house hundreds of LED lights, each designed to light up when members of the Royals homer. On those special occasions, the crown shines even more brightly than usual as the park's trademark fountains simultaneously erupt in celebration.

KAUFFMAN STADIUM

- Visit the **Negro Leagues Baseball Museum** (1616 E. 18th Street) and its Field of Legends, which displays statues of Buck O'Neil, Rube Foster, Josh Gibson, Satchel Paige, Cool Papa Bell, and other Negro Leagues stars
- Visit the **Royals Hall of Fame** behind sections 104-106 with its giant No. 5 made up of 3,154 baseballs, one for each of George Brett's career hits
- Play a round at the **baseball-themed minigolf course** at the Outfield Experience play area

BALLPARK BUCKET LIST

44 *Chicago Cubs*

THE ROOFTOP SEATS AT WRIGLEY FIELD

Visiting Wrigley Field, you can't help but feel as though you are watching a game at a neighborhood park. That holds true as you walk through the festive streets of Wrigleyville and as you settle into your ballpark seat and gaze at the rooftop hordes overlooking the outfield.

Through the decades, you could spot small groups of fans on the Wrigleyville roofs, firing up grills and unfolding lawn chairs, and the Cubs shrugged. After the team went to the National League Championship Series in 1984, though, their neighbors started building bleachers and charging admission, and the Cubs took offense. Defenders of the expensive rooftop clubs that emerged in the 1990s said Chicagoans had always watched games from the neighborhood, pointing to photos from the 1908 World Series as evidence. The Cubs argued rooftop club owners were profiting from their copyright-protected material.

Eventually, the sides reached an uneasy truce in 2004 when the abutters agreed to send 17 percent of rooftop ticket revenues to the team. After the Ricketts family bought the Cubs in 2009, though, tension mounted anew when the Cubs announced plans for a $575 million renovation that included two new outfield video boards and seven billboards, which would block rooftop views.

The club owners took the Cubs to court in 2015, claiming the obstructions violated the terms of their revenue-sharing agreement, but that September a federal judge dismissed the suit. By then, the Ricketts had begun buying the buildings with rooftop views, anyway, bringing them under team control. While most fans' natural reaction is to side with the little guy in confrontations like this, you have to admit the Wrigley rooftops ceased being mom-and-pop operations long ago. At least the Cubs stopped trying to put the kibosh on them and started investing in them. That guarantees they will remain a fixture of the Wrigley experience, and that's a good thing.

" *Ballpark Chatter* "

"The family continues to be interested in acquiring some of these buildings if there are owners who are interested in selling. It's going to be very helpful for fans. We're going to be able to create a variety of rooftop experiences for fans to choose from."

—DENNIS CULLOTON, RICKETTS FAMILY SPOKESPERSON IN 2016

The view from a Sheffield Avenue roof deck

The Pesky Pole, which gets signed
by fans in the pregame hour

THE PESKY POLE AT FENWAY PARK

Fenway Park's cherished right field landmark is closer to the plate than any other major-league foul pole, listing at 302 feet and rumored to be more like 295.

The pole's namesake, Johnny Pesky, was a smooth-fielding infielder who logged ten seasons with the Red Sox between 1942 and 1954. It was after he retired that he earned his "Mr. Red Sox" nickname, though, serving as Red Sox manager, broadcaster, first base coach, bench coach, batting coach, and spring training instructor. Even before Pesky became a beloved grandfatherly figure in Red Sox Nation, Boston fans took to calling Fenway's right field pole "the Pesky Pole," or "Pesky's Pole."

The man responsible for associating the pole with Pesky was former Red Sox pitcher Mel Parnell, who during his days as Red Sox broadcaster in the 1960s liked to recall a game in which the light-hitting Pesky earned him a win by slipping a late-inning homer around Fenway's right field pole. And whenever a ball flew toward the pole, Parnell would refer to it as "Pesky's Pole." The nickname stuck. There was only one problem: Parnell's recollection was faulty.

Pesky hit a grand total of 17 home runs in 5,515 big-league plate appearances. Six of those came at Fenway Park, but according to the baseball record books none came late in a game Parnell started. The closest such occurrence was an eighth-inning homer by Pesky in the Red Sox' 1946 home opener that helped Tex Hughson earn a 2–1 win against the A's. Only once did Pesky homer in a game Parnell pitched—in the first inning of a fourteen-inning loss to the Tigers in 1950.

Nonetheless, "Pesky's Pole" is etched in the vernacular of Red Sox fans and in bronze at the base of the pole itself. You may visit Fenway's right field boxes to see for yourself!

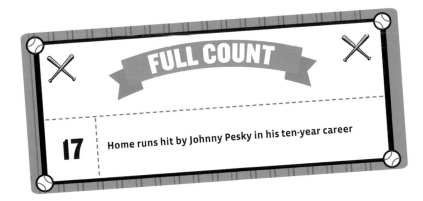

FULL COUNT

17 | Home runs hit by Johnny Pesky in his ten-year career

THE STEAM TRAIN AT MINUTE MAID PARK

Houston's historic Union Station does more than provide Minute Maid Park with a grand entrance; it also houses an old-fashioned steam engine on its roof. The prominently placed ballpark train replicates an 1860s-era locomotive as it runs from center field to left field along an 800-foot-long set of tracks.

Although the train is powered by electricity, it emits faux steam from its pipe as its 6-foot spoked wheels slowly turn. A bright red "cowcatcher" pushes stray steer from the tracks as well as any baseballs that get in the train's way. Counting the attached coal-tender's car—loaded with gigantic fake oranges—the assembly weighs almost 50,000 pounds.

MINUTE MAID PARK

- Visit the **statues of Craig Biggio and Jeff Bagwell** playing catch outside Union Station

- Pass through Union Station's **marble pillars** and **regal arches**

- Check out the **Home Run Pump**, which tallies the total homers hit at Minute Maid Park by the Astros since the park's opening

BALLPARK BUCKET LIST

Before the start of every game, the Astros' train slowly begins its first journey of the day as the final notes of the National Anthem fade into the Houston sky. Moving at 2 miles per hour, it takes a minute or so for it to reach the left field corner. Then, it drives in reverse to left-center and parks. Some 90 feet above the field, the train waits for a member of the Astros to hit a home run, whereupon it lurches into gear in celebration. After Astros wins, too, the train makes a journey across the outfield, blowing its whistle in triumph.

Since 2001, a man named Bobby Vasquez has been the train's conductor. Nicknamed "Bobby Dynamite," the affable Houstonian wears a set of blue overalls over an Astros T-shirt.

Through the years, plenty of balls have dinged the train, including one struck by the Brewers' Rickie Weeks that Vasquez nearly caught and another by Mariners slugger Nelson Cruz that prompted Vasquez to blow the train whistle in admiration (or surrender) even though it had been hit by a visitor.

The Minute Maid Park train—
which hauls, appropriately, a load
of oversized oranges—runs along
the top of historic Union Station.

The Rawhide Ballpark barn forms part of the right field fence behind pitcher Josh Collmenter, and even makes an impression from the air.

THE RED BARN AT RAWHIDE BALLPARK

In 2009, Visalia's California League team changed its name from Oaks to Rawhide—and built a big red barn in the right field power alley of its ballpark. The broadside of the barn forms a 40-foot stretch of the outfield wall.

The team's rebranding was meant to tie the club to its region's agricultural tradition, and the barn helps accomplish this. Located between Bakersfield and Fresno, Visalia lies in the heart of the fertile San Joaquin Valley, known for its grapes, olives, and citrus fruits. It is also a key player in the California dairy and livestock industries.

The barn serves as a supply shed for the grounds crew, while providing the outfield with a feature unlike any you will find elsewhere in baseball's bushes. Sitting in your ballpark seat, your eye is drawn to its bright red paint, sloped black roof, and two loft windows that together form an irregularly shaped and colored structure where you usually find a continuous expanse of outfield wall or outfield ads.

Standing some 365 feet from home plate, the 40-by-20-foot barn is just a pop fly from the "Pasture," a lawn seating area that begins in right field foul territory, wraps around the foul pole, and continues into home-run territory.

As you might expect, the Class-A players passing through Visalia get a kick out of the barn, taking aim at it when they step into the batter's box. If a player hits its side with a deep fly, the ball is in play and will likely go for a double. If the ball caroms off the black shingled roof, it is ruled a home run, even if it bounces back onto the field. The first player to smack a long ball completely over the structure was Ryan Wheeler, who dropped the horsehide into the kids play area behind the barn in 2010.

 Ballpark Chatter

"Neither of the pitchers could hit the broad side of a barn with the sphere, to say nothing of tackling it endwise."
—*EVENING NEWS* (SAGINAW, MICHIGAN) ARTICLE DESCRIBING A JUNE 1895 AMATEUR GAME, PENNING THE FIRST PUBLISHED EXAMPLE OF THIS IDIOM IN RELATION TO BASEBALL

48 Tulsa Drillers

THE OIL DERRICK AT ONEOK FIELD

Long before you reach ONEOK Field, you spot the 30-foot-tall oil derrick that stands at its right field entrance. Upon reaching it, you pass between its legs to access the ballpark concourse. Then, once you settle into your seat, you enjoy a view of the derrick all game long, reminding you that you're watching a game in the heart of oil country.

The derrick is a fitting tribute to Tulsa's identity. Before Houston supplanted it in the twentieth century, it was known as the "Oil Capital of the World," and the oil industry remains a vital part of its economy to this day. For years, the Drillers played at Oiler Park and Drillers Stadium, the names of which referenced the natural resource around which the city was built.

ONEOK Field replaced Drillers Stadium in 2010. The idea to incorporate a derrick into its design came from Populous architect Steve Boyd. Logically, the derrick might have been placed at the home plate gate, which is usually a park's most prominent entrance, but because ONEOK Field's grandstand was built nearly abutting Interstate 244, Boyd and his peers decided to create several entrances around the entire field rather than channeling fans into a main entrance in tight quarters. As such, you find entrances at home plate, first base, left field, center field, and right field—where the oil derrick stands at the corner of Elgin Avenue and Archer Street.

If you are looking to snap off the quintessential Tulsa Drillers selfie, the latter is the easy choice. At night, its blue and white lights illuminate the Drillers' "T," which comes complete with a drip of oil hanging from the bottom of the dipstick.

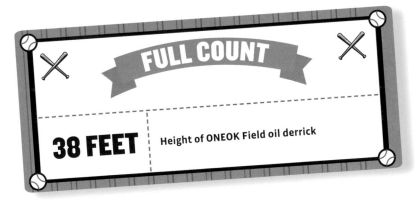

FULL COUNT

38 FEET | Height of ONEOK Field oil derrick

Having passed beneath the derrick, fans enjoy a game followed by fireworks.

There is no more beautiful sight in baseball than the sun setting on the Wasatch Mountains beyond Smith's Ballpark.

THE MOUNTAIN VIEWS AT SMITH'S BALLPARK

For the most breathtaking mountain views in all the major or minor leagues, you must set your road-trip-car's GPS for Salt Lake City, Utah, where you find a baseball setting fit for the gods. If the big ball field in the sky to which baseball immortals report upon leaving this world doesn't look something like Smith's Ballpark, it ought to.

The home of the Salt Lake Bees showcases the beautiful Wasatch Mountains beyond its left and center field walls. Perhaps the locals eventually get used to such amazing displays of Mother Nature's grandeur, but as a visitor from afar, you will likely find the view so mesmerizing that you have difficulty keeping your eyes on the game.

Composing the western edge of the Rockies, the Wasatch peaks are still snow-covered when baseball season begins, but lose their frost by summer. As the setting sun shines on them, they turn a pinkish hue that makes an already breathtaking sight all the more arresting. Just as the famous big-league park in Baltimore has its warehouse, the park in San Francisco has its sparkling blue sea, and the park in Pittsburgh has its downtown skyline, Salt Lake City has its mountains . . . and they are spectacular.

Because the Wasatch Range is most glorious beyond the left field side of the park, sitting on the first base side of Smith's Ballpark is highly recommended. And Smith's is one park where you shouldn't even think about sitting on the outfield berm, which positions you with your back to the amazing view all game long.

" *Ballpark Chatter* "

"The mountains are calling and I must go."

—JOHN MUIR, NATURALIST

GREENE'S HILL AT GLOBE LIFE PARK IN ARLINGTON

Watching a home run touch down on Globe Life Park's sloped center field lawn is a pleasure to behold. After all, who doesn't enjoy witnessing a youngster's excitement upon snagging a big-league ball? Even if you have never had the good fortune of scooping up a ball of your own, you can probably recall a time when your childhood dreams entertained such notions. And you can live vicariously through the kiddos' joy when you visit Arlington.

When balls land on Globe Life Park's batter's eye, the scramble begins, and it doesn't end until one of the kids emerges with the ball held high. If struck by the Rangers, the ball becomes a cherished souvenir. If one of the visitors knocked it out of the park, it may well be heaved back onto the field.

While Globe Life Park is a decidedly hitter-friendly park, not every venture into its stands will include your witnessing a home-run scramble on Greene's Hill, but if you arrive early, you can watch the kids shag balls on the hill during batting practice, which is almost as delightful a spectacle.

Named after former Arlington mayor Richard Greene, who championed the park's construction in the 1990s, the hill is off limits 99.99 percent of the time. But as soon as the horsehide lands on Greene's Hill, you can jump the railing that separates it from the right or left field seats.

If you are a Rangers fan, the faces you see on the hill become familiar over the course of a season. One super-fan has amassed a cult following thanks to his prowess at scooping balls off the hill, or even catching them on the fly. Trent Williams (aka "The Greene's Hill Kid") puts on a pretty good show.

GLOBE LIFE PARK

- Visit the **outfield statue** depicting Nolan Ryan raising his cap to salute the Texas fans after recording his seventh no-hitter, against the Blue Jays in 1991
- Watch the **"Rangers Six-Shooters" cheerleading squad** dance atop the dugouts while "Cotton Eye Joe" plays in the middle of the seventh
- Stop by the **Texas Rangers Hall of Fame** in right field, which chronicles the team's history since arriving in Arlington in 1972

BALLPARK BUCKET LIST

Greene's Hill often lies vacant. But it doesn't when a home-run ball touches down on its grass, setting off a mad scramble. Pictured here, members of the Texas Army National Guard hold the Texas State flag on Greene's Hill prior to Game Four of the 2011 World Series.

The Grandstand Seats

THE WOODEN GRANDSTAND SEATS AT FENWAY PARK

Fenway Park's wooden grandstand seats are one of its most authentic and endearing features. Sitting on the blue wooden slats with your elbows resting on cast iron armrests, you can't help but think that you are experiencing a game as your forefathers did during the Classic Ballpark Era. It is pretty amazing to think that your fanny rests on the very pieces of oak that welcomed the rooters who cheered for Jimmie Foxx, Ted Williams, Carl Yastrzemski, and the other legends who have graced the Fenway lawn since its grandstand benches were replaced with seats in the 1930s.

These are the only wooden seats left in Major League Baseball, and despite what pampered modern fans may think of their lack of posterior padding, they are a treasure. To put in perspective just how remarkable it is that these seats have endured, consider that Oriole Park's seats, which were regaled as the most comfortable in baseball when that park opened in 1992, didn't last even two decades. The Orioles ripped out the last of them prior to the 2011 season and replaced them with wider ones that include built-in cupholders.

At Fenway, you put your soda between your thighs like your grandfather did when he watched a game. You stand up and suck in your gut when someone in your row needs to access the concession stand or bathroom. And you stand and stretch in the middle of the seventh inning not because it's a ballpark custom, but because your back and knees need the reprieve.

In fairness, Fenway's wooden seats are more comfortable today than they were a generation ago. The Red Sox refurbished them between 2009 and 2011, repairing broken slats, repainting them, adding springs to raise the lower halves when they aren't occupied, and widening most of them from 15 to 18 inches.

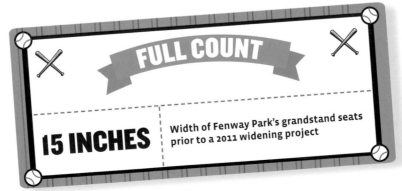

FULL COUNT

15 INCHES — Width of Fenway Park's grandstand seats prior to a 2011 widening project

★ SEALS STADIUM ★
MAJOR LEAGUE BASEBALL'S FIRST WEST COAST GAME, APRIL 15, 1958

Upon relocating from New York to California in 1958, the Dodgers and Giants established temporary residencies at Los Angeles Memorial Coliseum and Seals Stadium, respectively. Seals Stadium hosted the big leagues' first West Coast game on April 15, 1958, as the Giants downed Don Drysdale and the Dodgers, 8–0, before 23,448 fans. Over the shoulder of Dodgers catcher Al Walker is the legendary Hamm's Brewery sign. The 13-foot-tall chalice filled and emptied with rings of light!

SEALING A PLACE IN BASEBALL HISTORY

- Seals Stadium opened in 1931 to provide a home to San Francisco's two Pacific Coast League teams: the Seals and Missions. It offered three clubhouses; one for each home team, and one for the visitors.

- In 1933, 18-year-old Joe DiMaggio hit safely in 61 straight games for the Seals on his way to posting a .340 batting average and 169 RBI.

52 *Colorado Rockies*

THE OUTFIELD FOREST AT COORS FIELD

Coors Field's forest began in straightaway center field, but through the years has invaded the abutting right field bullpens. The natural growth makes the forest look all the more authentic and beautiful. It includes dozens of small evergreens and deciduous trees, as well as many of the shrubs and flowers common to Colorado's mountainsides. In the middle of the attraction, the ice-melt from some unseen peak trickles over ruby red sandstone boulders into a mountain pool. Seven geysers erupt when the Rockies take the field in the top of the first inning, when they hit a home run, and when they get ready to bat as fans celebrate the seventh-inning stretch.

There is no wall separating the forest from the visitors' bullpen, and the vegetation has filled in the spaces surrounding the patch of lawn over which pitchers and catchers toss the ball. Trees grow along the back and front of the pen, and when a ball gets past a bullpen catcher, it means somebody is going to have to go trouncing into the woods.

On a hot day in August 2015, Mariners closer Fernando Rodney memorably picked up one of the folding chairs in the bullpen and carried it into a dense stand of forest. Barely visible to the TV cameras, Rodney watched a few innings through the foliage before being summoned to pitch and promptly giving up the lead. After the Mariners lost, critics in Seattle suggested that perhaps he was not taking the game seriously enough.

Later that season, in September 2015, Padres relievers took to the forest to scour the landscape for rookie Tom Murphy's first career home run, which they eventually located among the river rocks.

" *Ballpark Chatter* "

"We're not sure if it was an escape from the blinding Colorado sun on a hot day or an impromptu game of peek-a-boo but Mariners closer Fernando Rodney was the talk of Twitter after a mysterious jaunt into the 'woods' behind the bullpen."

—KIMA-TV, CENTRAL WASHINGTON, NEWS REPORT

The forest in center field creeps into the right field bullpens, and the geysers in the batter's eye send water shooting into the air.

Parents sit in the bleachers while children play in the sand, where creative fans made a sculpture of the Padres' Friar in 2011.

THE BEACH AT PETCO PARK

While it may seem frivolous to devote prime real estate in home-run territory to what amounts to a giant sandbox, in San Diego, where the beach is woven into the civic fabric, it makes perfect sense.

The Petco Park Beach lies behind the chain-link outfield fence in right-center, stocked with shovels, buckets, sifters, and other toys. During batting practice, anyone can visit to make a castle or dig a hole. Once the game begins, the area is restricted to those fans holding bleacher tickets. If you are catching a game with a youngster who ordinarily lacks the attention span to sit through the full nine innings, the area presents an ideal way to extend your visit. You may play in the sand too, if you like, or you may take a seat in the abutting bleachers.

Petco Park also offers the major leagues' only grass seating berm. The 2.7-acre hillside rises behind the Beach, attracting baby-strolling moms and dads, twentysomethings toting beach blankets, and couples carrying picnic baskets and coolers. You read that right: Outside food is permitted at the Park at the Park, as well as water bottles and juice boxes.

The only knock on the Park at the Park is that the view it offers is partially obstructed by the batter's eye in center field. You enjoy the best looks from the top of the hillside.

Both Petco Park's sandy Beach and grassy Park at the Park provide special San Diegan ways to enjoy a game. You should sample them at least once to expand your idea of what a ballpark experience can be. Then, you can go back to scouring StubHub for seats in the infield boxes.

PETCO PARK

- Visit the **Tony Gwynn statue** at the back of the Park at the Park

- Sample the beef brisket at the **Randy Jones BBQ stand** on the first level concourse

- Listen for the **whistle** from the **USS *Ronald Reagan*** whenever the Padres hit a home run

BALLPARK BUCKET LIST

54 *Arizona Diamondbacks*

THE KEYHOLE AT CHASE FIELD

When Chase Field was being designed in the mid-1990s, a wave of futuristic new ballparks seemed poised to splash across the United States, ushering America's Game into the twenty-first century. SkyDome had opened in Toronto in 1989, and hordes of baseball tourists had responded by making a pilgrimage to the Great White North. Fortunately, Oriole Park opened less than three years later, and there soon emerged a groundswell of enthusiasm for ballparks that recalled the intimacy and grandeur of baseball's past. This abrupt pivot left the expansion Arizona Diamondbacks in a quandary. On the one hand, the team needed to safeguard its fans and players against the 100-degree Phoenix temps. On the other hand, the team recognized that fans were suddenly enamored with old-time parks.

In response, the Diamondbacks gave their ultra-modern facility a throwback effect that none of the other retro parks had included: a dirt runway connecting the pitcher's mound and batter's circle. The 50-foot strip was the only one of its kind when Phoenix's new yard opened; it was copied two years later when Comerica Park opened in Detroit.

As a perusal of old photos will confirm, these strips were once found throughout the game, each combining with the mound and batter's circle to create a red clay pattern called a "keyhole." Historians are unsure whether the paths were inspired by the dirt strip on a cricket field, or whether they were the result of contemporary grounds crews' inability to keep up with the foot traffic between home plate and the mound. Whichever was the case, by the 1950s the last of them had disappeared . . . until the Diamondbacks resurrected a forgotten ballpark nuance and in so doing gave their futuristic park a delightful old-time touch.

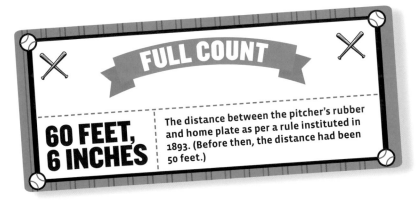

FULL COUNT

60 FEET, 6 INCHES

The distance between the pitcher's rubber and home plate as per a rule instituted in 1893. (Before then, the distance had been 50 feet.)

The dirt path between the pitcher's mound and batter's box joins those other dirt patches to form a pattern known as a "keyhole."

The multicolored seats at CHS Field reflect the quirky aesthetic sensibilities of the Twin Cities.

THE FUNKY SEATS AT CHS FIELD

CHS Field offers a design nuance characteristic of many Twin Cities gathering spaces. If you arrive just as the game is beginning, when the seating bowl is already full, you will fail to notice it. If you arrive at least a half hour before the first pitch, though, or wait until most fans have exited the seating bowl after the game, you will surely be taken by the multiple shades of gray and randomly placed gold seats that fill the stands.

Plenty of other ballparks offer a variety of seat colors, but they group them in separate seating areas, such as Fenway Park, which has red Field Box seats, blue Grandstand seats, and green Bleacher seats, or Dodger Stadium, which offers a different hue on each deck. At CHS Field, the different colors mix together, creating an artsy effect that is one-of-a-kind in the baseball world.

While the Saints deserve props for introducing this quirky approach to seating to baseball fans, performance centers and arenas in their parts have featured multicolored seating decks for generations. Minneapolis's Guthrie Theatre at Vineland Place offers a kaleidoscope of purple, mauve, gold, and turquoise around its thrust stage. Bloomington's Metropolitan Sports Center, home to the NHL's Minnesota North Stars from 1967 to 1993, offered stands that looked like the inside of a crayon box, with a mish mash of white, yellow, green, and gray.

All of this is to say that the funky seats at CHS Field fit into a larger regional tradition. For bucking baseball's usual way of doing things and reflecting their community's quirky sensibility, the Saints deserve a tip of the cap.

CHS FIELD

- Get a backrub at **Sister Rosalind's concourse massage stand**

- Cheer for the **pot-bellied pig** that delivers fresh game balls to the home plate umpire

- Check out the **300 outfield solar panels** that provide 12 percent of the park's electricity

BALLPARK BUCKET LIST

San Francisco Giants

THE CABLE CAR AT AT&T PARK

San Francisco's cable cars are one of its main tourist attractions, ranking right up there with the Golden Gate Bridge and Alcatraz Island on most visitors' hit lists. Fittingly, then, you find a retired car on AT&T Park's right-center field concourse.

Not to be confused with trolley cars or streetcars, which are powered by different mechanisms entirely, cable cars were invented by San Franciscan Andrew Smith Hallidie in 1873. They are pulled by underground cables that run between their rails. Once, they could be found in cities across the United States, but today you only find them in San Francisco.

At the height of their popularity, San Francisco's cable cars traveled along twenty-three lines, shuttling commuters and shoppers up and down the city's infamous hills. Although most locals today choose other modes of transportation, the forty remaining cars are a point of civic pride.

The ballpark cable car offers views of McCovey Cove on one side and of the field on the other. You can stand on its rails or sit on its wooden benches. To board one of the city's operational cable cars, you have to endure long lines and fork over six dollars for a short ride. To check out AT&T Park's car—labeled No. 44 in homage to Willie McCovey, who wore that number for nineteen seasons—you need only take a midgame stroll out to right field.

The car is even equipped with an authentic bell that—in keeping with a tradition established when the Pacific Coast League's San Francisco Seals were the only show in town—rings out the number of runs the home team has at the conclusion of each inning.

" *Ballpark Chatter* "

"It's a token of gratitude."

—JAKE PEAVY, ON PURCHASING A TROLLEY CAR FOR HIS
ALABAMA HOME AFTER WINNING THE 2014 WORLD SERIES
WITH THE GIANTS

Fans can watch the game from the Giants' cable car, or enjoy the sweeping views of McCovey Cove and AT&T Park.

Fans drop lines over the first base dugout, and a young fan fishes over the third base dugout.

THE FISHING RAILS AT MCCOY STADIUM

You may travel far and wide in pursuit of ballpark bliss, but only in Pawtucket, Rhode Island, will you encounter a ballpark fishing wharf, or rather a pair of them, tempting anglers. Indeed, in the pregame hour you spy many young fans casting lines from the McCoy Stadium stands. Some use rigs from home, others use fishing kits purchased at the ballpark concession stands. If you are traveling with a youngster, you are strongly encouraged to partake. Who knows, you might just hook a whopper, maybe the next Mike Trout, Tim Salmon, Catfish Hunter, Kevin Bass, Gil Hodges, or Mike Carp . . . or, at the very least, a Cole Sturgeon.

That's right, you don't cast for fish at McCoy Stadium but for autographs. And your best chance of heading home with a keeper . . . err . . . keepsake . . . doesn't come from *handing* your baseball cards and Sharpie to the players but from arriving with a fishing line and *lowering* them down to the field. That's because when McCoy Stadium was constructed in the early 1940s, it was designed with the dugouts at field level. This decision placed the first row of seats about 8 feet above the playing surface, making it pretty much impossible for fans to reach out and high-five or hand a pen to players. To their credit, autograph hounds in Pawtucket found another way to get the job done.

Prior to your visit, find an empty gallon jug and cut out one side, leaving the handle in place. Next, affix a 6-foot rope to the handle. Once you get to the park, head to the railing above the first base (visitors) or third base (home) dugout, put a ball or some baseball cards in the carton, and lower it down to the players' waist level.

Happy fishing!

" *Ballpark Chatter* "

"Not too many times do you walk into a stadium and people are hanging down milk cartons with balls in them to have you sign."

—RICH GEDMAN, FORMER PAWTUCKET AND BOSTON RED SOX CATCHER

THE RIVERBOAT AND POWER STACKS AT GREAT AMERICAN BALL PARK

For more than three decades the Cincinnati Reds played in a ballpark that offered nary a glimpse of the Ohio River rolling past. Despite being known as Riverfront Stadium for much of its life, the Reds' home was sealed in from the outside by three decks of seating. Thankfully, Great American Ball Park opened in 2003 to offer gorgeous views of the Ohio across its outfield. And to complete the river theme, the Reds installed a giant riverboat and two tall power stacks that rise from the outfield stands.

From the decks of the big boat, you can survey the river, the Taylor Southgate Bridge, and Covington, Kentucky. You can also see the downtown Cincinnati skyline rising behind the home plate grandstand. Each night, the riverboat serves as a festive group party area, offering 7,500 square feet of deck space to parties of 20 to 150 people.

To the right of the party vessel, the two power stacks rise 64 feet into the sky. They bear decorative paddlewheels on their bases and light up at night. Each stack is crowned with seven bats. Seven plus seven equals 14, of course, which was the number worn by Reds legend Pete Rose.

The power stacks do more than merely standing there and looking pretty. When a Reds pitcher strikes out a batter, fire flares from their tops. When a Reds batter hits a home run or the Reds finish off a win, they spew fireworks. On hot days, they spray mist into the air to cool the fans in the nearby Sun Deck.

When properly functioning, the stacks are a ballpark treasure. On May 15, 2015, however, they caused a bit of a problem when the right stack caught on fire after erupting to celebrate a Billy Hamilton home run. The Cincinnati Fire Department had to extinguish the blaze.

FULL COUNT

981 MILES | Length of the Ohio River

A ring of bats encircles each of the Reds' power stacks, and the riverboat rises above the black center field batter's eye.

As rays glide through the water, fans feed and pet them, and pose for the ultimate Tropicana Field photo.

THE RAYS TOUCH TANK AT TROPICANA FIELD

In a town where the fans don't always support the home team to the degree you might expect, the Rays Touch Tank provides a shimmering oasis amid the catwalks, artificial turf, and empty seats. The kid-friendly attraction scores points for its ease of access and for playing off the home team's identity so nicely.

You find the 35-by-20-foot tank's bubbling waters in right-center field home-run territory at Tropicana Field, stocked with about thirty cownose rays. The majestic fish seem to glide through the water as they flap their fins. They eat mostly squid and shellfish and like to be petted.

As soon as the ballpark gates open, you can visit the tank via the outfield concourse at no cost beyond what you paid for your game ticket. You can stand tank-side and watch the rays fly through the water, or, for a small donation, can purchase some squid to drop into the tank. Only fifty fans at a time are allowed to access the tank's edges, and the ballpark staff does a good job of making sure everyone interested in playing with the fish gets a chance. If the tank is too crowded before the game, the attendant gives you a ticket stamped with a time when you can return for an "appointment" with the fish a bit later in the day.

The tank also provides a distant splash-landing target for hitters. From the tank's installation in 2006 through 2015, only the Dodgers' Luis Gonzalez (2007), the Tigers' Miguel Cabrera (2013), the Rays' Jose Lobaton (2013 American League Division Series walk-off), and the Mariners' Nelson Cruz (2015 game-winner) have reached the saltwater.

For the record, baseballs float in the Rays Touch Tank, just as they do at McCovey Cove in San Francisco.

" Ballpark Chatter "

"We were tied to the past, and the past wasn't necessarily something we wanted to be known for. . . . I hope and expect the fans who come out will see it as a new beginning."
—STUART STERNBERG, RAYS OWNER, EXPLAINING THE DECISION TO DROP DEVIL FROM THE TEAM'S NICKNAME IN 2007

THE GIANT COKE BOTTLE AT COCA-COLA PARK

Coca-Cola Park features a ballpark adornment that would surely bring a smile even to the dour face of legendary baseball grump Ty Cobb, who was an early pitchman for and investor in Coca-Cola. The home of the Lehigh Valley IronPigs pays tribute to the quintessential American soda brand with a giant Coke bottle mounted atop its outfield scoreboard. The bottle is not only an advertisement, but also a celebration machine that, when shaken, does what soda bottles tend to do: It explodes!

When the IronPigs score a run, the bottle lights up, vibrates, and then emits a spray of fizz. When they hit a home run, its cap flips open and fizz erupts in the form of colorful fireworks.

While you may have a visceral resistance to embracing a corporate emblem as ballpark art, it is important to remember that outfield walls and scoreboards have donned company logos since the game's early days, so two-dimensional advertising at the ballpark is old hat. You may also recall that similarly three-dimensional Coke bottles were once part of the outfield skylines at Fenway Park and Turner Field, and that there is still a giant Coke bottle in the left field stands at AT&T Park. And out of all those bottles, the one at Coca-Cola Park adds the most to the game-day experience.

The bottle also fits in eastern Pennsylvania, where Coke is clearly no carpetbagger. The Coca-Cola Bottling Company of Lehigh Valley has been part of the local economy since its founding in Bethlehem in 1917.

Whether you opt to buy a Coca-Cola, Sprite, Powerade, or one of the other Coke products they sell at the Coca-Cola Park stands, or just drink bubbler water, you should enjoy the big bottle's theatrics when fate smiles on the IronPigs.

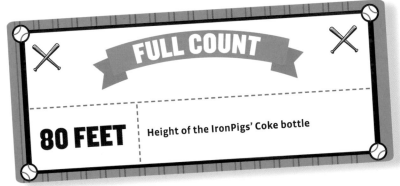

FULL COUNT

80 FEET : Height of the IronPigs' Coke bottle

The Coke bottle atop the scoreboard rises nearly as high as the light towers and shoots fireworks when the IronPigs have occasion to celebrate.

The JetBlue Monster in the pregame hour, and with fans watching the game from within it and atop it

THE GREEN MONSTER SEATS AT JETBLUE PARK

You will find Green Monster replicas at minor-league ballparks up and down the East Coast, but to visit the most unusual Fenway-inspired wall of all, you must travel to the southernmost tip of Red Sox Nation—Fort Myers, Florida, where the Red Sox spring training home offers its own twist on the Monster meme.

At JetBlue Park you may not only sit *atop* the towering left field wall, but you may also watch a game from *inside* it. The Fort Myers Monster offers three rows of pavilion-style seating midway up its 43-foot-high face. The seats are tucked safely behind the same type of protective netting you find safeguarding fans behind home plate backstops. As you watch a game from one of the 258 seats inside the wall, you enjoy the surreal experience of seeing screaming line drives come right toward you until they spring off the netting or thud against the wall above or below.

Not only do these unusually placed seats offer you a unique viewing experience, but they also create a one-of-a-kind backdrop for a game for those who choose to sit elsewhere in the park. The effect is similar to watching a game at Fenway . . . after all, there is a big green wall in left field with a manually operated scoreboard and seats up top, and there are replicas of Fenway's famous center field triangle, the Pesky Pole, and Fenway's red seat in right field. But there are people inside the wall in Fort Myers, which gives the park its own special eccentricity.

If you visit Fort Myers in March, during the spring training season, a seat inside the wall costs about the same as one in the infield boxes. Another option is to catch a game at JetBlue Park during the Gulf Coast League Red Sox's season, which starts in mid-June each year.

JET BLUE PARK

- Check out the **detached JetBlue tailfin** that serves as a sundial outside the park

- Stroll through the **monument park** that sprouts the giant red numbers once worn by Red Sox legends like Ted Williams, Carl Yastrzemski, and Wade Boggs

- Order a **Fenway Frank** that tastes just as good as the ones they serve in Boston

BALLPARK BUCKET LIST

62 *Lakewood BlueClaws*

THE LIFEGUARD CHAIRS AT FIRSTENERGY PARK

Although Lakewood is not located right at the water's edge, it is in Ocean County, and, as such, embraces its region's Jersey Shore identity. The association between team and beach took a big step forward in 2002 when former BlueClaws general manager Geoff Brown came up with the idea to host a Beach Night at FirstEnergy Park. As part of the promotion, the team installed a lifeguard chair beyond the outfield fence that fans could visit and sit in. The chair proved to be such a hit that afterward the BlueClaws contracted a local handyman to make the five chairs you find spanning the outfield of their park today.

Set atop the outfield seating lawn, the chairs may look identical to the ones you find sprouting from the sand at your favorite beach. But upon closer inspection you will notice they are wider than the typical lifeguard chair and easier to mount thanks to their kid-friendly rungs that start a foot above the ground.

Each chair is wide enough to allow four or five youngsters to sit side-by-side watching the game from high above the field. Although each rises only about 7 feet, it seems higher thanks to its placement atop the outfield berm, which crests 20 feet above the warning track.

You will find two chairs in left field home-run territory and three in right, set between the large billboards that seal in FirstEnergy Park from the outside world. Through the years, they have taken incoming fire from heavy-hitting sluggers on occasion, most memorably in 2011 when Jim Murphy knocked two dingers off the chairs on his way to hitting twenty-two long balls to establish the BlueClaws' single-season record.

So, bring your glove, your sunscreen and some orange trunks, and enjoy a baseball experience unique to the Jersey Shore!

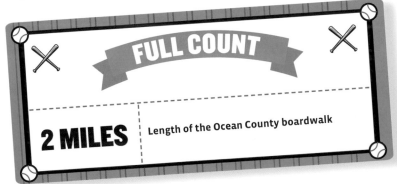

FULL COUNT

2 MILES — Length of the Ocean County boardwalk

The lifeguard chairs—
where fans can watch
the game—rise
from the back of the
outfield berm.

The Twins' retired numbers hang above the limestone wall in left field foul territory.

THE YELLOW LIMESTONE AT TARGET FIELD

The Minnesota Twins gave Target Field a distinctly Minnesotan flair when they selected the yellow sedimentary rock known as Kasota lime to adorn their park's home plate backstop. The Twins didn't stop there, though, as the slabs of the pretty yellow rock cover pretty much every other open space at Target Field too. More artsy than concrete but less prim-and-proper than red brick, the limestone complements the park's green stadium seats and green lawn just perfectly.

Mined by the Vetter Stone Company in southern Minnesota, the dolomite-rich rock is popular throughout the Gopher State and across the Midwest. The Minnesota State capitol—across the river in St. Paul—uses Kasota lime throughout its interior; PNC Park in Pittsburgh uses the rock in its exterior. At Target Field, where even the door handles take the shape of the state of Minnesota, one can imagine it was an easy choice to feature this homegrown stone.

As you approach the ballpark, you are greeted by a yellow facade that also incorporates glass and steel to create a chic exterior. This is not the retro look of a generation ago. This is something new. On the ballpark façade and everywhere else the stone appears, the variance between the different slabs' shades of yellow gives the park a funky look.

Inside, you find the most prominent displays of the limestone atop the dugout roofs, on the large wall that rises in left field foul territory, and on the field-facing side of the right field home-run territory seats that hang out over the warning track.

Of course, any open-air park would have been a vast improvement over the Twins' former home, the Metrodome, but thanks to the infusion of this beautiful yellow limestone, the Twins' home feels all the more warm and inviting. And those qualities go a long way in the often chilly Upper Midwest.

TARGET FIELD

- Visit the **Mall of America** in nearby Bloomington and find the home plate from the Twins' first home, Metropolitan Stadium, in its original location
- Find the **Gold Glove sculpture on Target Plaza** honoring Jim Kaat, who won eleven of his sixteen Gold Glove Awards with the Twins
- Peruse **Target Plaza's statues** of favorite Twins like Kirby Puckett, Harmon Killebrew, Rod Carew, and Tony Oliva

BALLPARK BUCKET LIST

★ GREENLEE FIELD, PITTSBURGH ★ CRAWFORDS, 1932–1938

In 1932, Pittsburgh Crawfords owner Gus Greenlee opened baseball's first African-American-owned ballpark. Buoyed by the prominent nightclub owner's bankroll, the Crawfords fielded some of the best Negro Leagues teams ever assembled over the next seven years, featuring lineups that included Cool Papa Bell, Oscar Charleston, Josh Gibson, Judy Johnson, and Satchel Paige.

GREENLEE AND THE NEGRO LEAGUES

- After building his park in six months, Gus Greenlee rode onto the field in a red convertible to throw out the ceremonial first pitch on the date of the stadium's grand opening.

- Satchel Paige started the first game at Greenlee Field, pitching to catcher Josh Gibson against the New York Black Yankees.

- Historians consider the 1935 Crawfords—who won the Negro National League championship—one of the best Negro Leagues teams ever assembled.

Champion Negro National League
1935

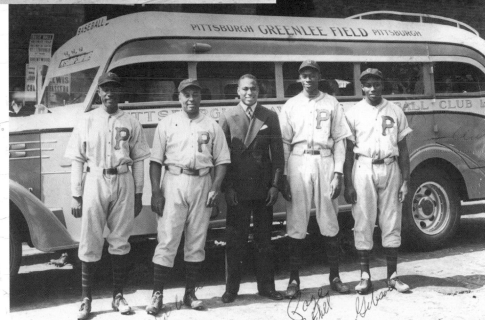

64 *New York Mets*

SHEA BRIDGE AT CITI FIELD

Shea Stadium's upper deck was steep and towering. Its outfield dimensions were symmetrical. Its color scheme was orange, blue, and concrete, and not necessarily in that order. And it was plopped in the midst of a baseball wasteland that offered few peripheral attractions for fans. And yet, it was where the Miracle Mets defied the odds to win the 1969 World Series, where the Mets of 1973, 1986, and 2000 likewise made World Series runs, where a super-fan named "The Sign Man" treated his fellow rooters to witty works of wordplay, and where the Home Run Apple blossomed.

While it may not have been *much* of a baseball park, to Mets fans it was *their* baseball park, and its demolition was bittersweet. Wisely, then, when the Mets designed Citi Field, they incorporated within it a lasting tribute to both Shea Stadium and its namesake.

Strolling Citi Field's first-level concourse, you eventually come upon this special ballpark feature in right-center field in the form of a wide pedestrian bridge modeled after a steel highway overpass. You can merely cross Shea Bridge and continue on your way, or you can stop midway across it and watch the game for a while.

The bridge honors William A. Shea, the New York attorney who followed an unconventional path to bring National League ball back to New York after the Dodgers and Giants headed west. In 1959 Shea announced his intention to form the Continental League, with teams in five cities including New York. The fledgling circuit disbanded in 1960, but not before Major League Baseball announced that two of its prospective cities—Houston and New York—would receive National League expansion teams.

Today, you can enjoy a game played against the backdrop of Shea Bridge, which honors the Mets' previous home as well as the man who ushered the team into existence.

" *Ballpark Chatter* "

**"A new stadium is costly.
You have to get your money somewhere."**

—BILL SHEA JR., ON THE METS INKING A $400 MILLION, TWENTY-YEAR
NAMING RIGHTS DEAL WITH CITIGROUP AFTER THEIR PREVIOUS HOME
HAD BEEN NAMED AFTER HIS FATHER

Fans can walk along Shea Bridge or watch the game from it.

The buildings of downtown Charlotte seem just a long flyball away during this college game played at BB&T Ballpark between the Charlotte 49ers and N.C. State Wolfpack in 2016.

THE SKYLINE AT BB&T BALLPARK

You won't find a more gorgeous city skyline on display across a ballpark outfield than the one that sparkles just beyond the fences at BB&T Ballpark. The crisp, clean contours of more than a dozen Charlotte skyscrapers form a beautiful backdrop for a game. If it looks as if the downtown buildings are rising from *just* beyond the ballpark grounds, that's because they are. From the seats you can see the Bank of America Center and Carillon Tower in right field, the Duke Energy Center on the first base side, and several other hallmarks of the local cityscape.

This amazing view has been on display since 2014 when the Queen City's new park opened on a plot that had at first been considered too small to accommodate minor-league ball. The architects at Odell Associates, Inc. could have been scared off by the two-block canvas, but instead they used it to paint a masterpiece. They oriented the field facing northeast to show off the tall buildings, and used the tiny footprint as an excuse to bend or even break some of the traditional rules associated with ballpark design, putting the fences closer to home plate than usual—especially in right field where a ball only needs to travel 315 feet to plop into the home-run porch. The foul territory is minimal. The concourses feature portable concession carts in lieu of the expansive built-in counters you find at most other parks.

As nice as these other quirks are, the skyline is what really defines BB&T Ballpark. Whether you are sitting along the third base line, behind home plate, or even in the narrow band of seats in the left field power alley, you can't help but gaze at the looming structures ringing the park. The buildings dwarf the scoreboard, the 18-foot-tall dragon in left-center field, and the ballpark light towers.

 Ballpark Chatter

"There's an old saying that constraint is an architect's best friend. When you have constraints, it drives a unique solution to respond to those constraints."

—MIKE WOLLEN, ODELL ASSOCIATES MANAGING PRINCIPAL

66 *Miami Marlins*

THE AQUATIC BACKSTOP AT MARLINS PARK

Believe it or not, when Marlins Park was being conceived, the Marlins actually toyed with the idea of building into the outfield fence a large tank and stocking it with sharks or marlins. Imagine, an outfielder drifting back to track a long flyball, reaching out a hand for the wall, and a shark snapping at his hand on the other side of the glass! But alas, the Marlins eventually decided to honor their aquatic identity with two smaller tanks on either side of the home plate backstop at Marlins Park.

Each tank measures 24 feet long and holds 450 gallons of water. If you are sitting in the first row of the Diamond Club, your feet are on the same level as the tank's sandy bottom. You can lean down and experience a distorted view of the field through the water and two panes of 1.5-inch shatterproof glass, or you can just look over the tank and watch the game.

The hundred or so fish that occupy these unique ballpark habitats dart between coral and decorative plants while treating fans and players alike to a most unusual ballpark frill. The tanks house species typically found in the warm waters off South Florida. They were installed in time for Opening Day 2012 after being constructed by a Fort Lauderdale aquarium company. As a safeguard against the potential horror of a foul ball, flying bat, or front row fan's knee shattering a tank and sending hundreds of gallons of water and flopping fish onto the field, the Marlins had first baseman Gaby Sanchez test the tanks' strength by firing 80-mile-per-hour "fastballs" at the glass a few days before the park's inaugural game. The tanks passed the test and have been Marlins Park's signature feature ever since.

MARLINS PARK

- Follow the **colorful tiled pathways** that lead to the stadium gates
- Ponder the **orange letters** on the park's east plaza **from the sign for the Orange Bowl**, which once stood on the ballpark site
- Enjoy the view of the beautiful Miami skyline through the park's enormous **left field window**

BALLPARK BUCKET LIST

The Marlins' fish tanks photographed during a pregame ballpark tour, as the Cubs' Alfonso Soriano takes a mighty cut in 2012, and as the Cubs' Starlin Castro approaches the batter's box in 2011.

The sun is always shining on the center field California Spectacular.

THE CALIFORNIA SPECTACULAR AT ANGEL STADIUM OF ANAHEIM

Thanks to its location, Angel Stadium of Anaheim is often a director's first choice when it comes time to film a ballpark scene. But just as the ballpark has left its mark on the silver screen, Hollywood has left a mark on it. During the six years the Walt Disney Company owned the Angels, the studio plopped a gargantuan movie prop behind the left-center field fence.

The aptly named California Spectacular creates a fitting backdrop for a game being played on the outskirts of Hollywood. And although the stadium is surrounded by strip malls, parking lots, and freeways, if you suspend your disbelief, you find yourself transported to an idyllic little park at the foot of a rocky mountain.

The rocks at the top of the formation make a capital A, through which a stream trickles. Down below, the center field cameramen ply their trade from within a cozy cave. The hillside also recalls California's Yosemite National Park, offering geysers that erupt on cue—often accompanied by fireworks.

Further contributing to the rustic illusion, ivy climbs up the sides of the mountain and palm trees grow at its foot. These are real palms, although the grass from which they sprout is artificial. The fake grass also sprouts flagpoles flying red and white pennants in honor of the Angels teams that have made the playoffs since the team's founding in 1961.

The California Spectacular was unveiled in 1998 as one of the final touches on an Angel Stadium renovation. Suddenly, a field that had been enclosed offered views of the Santa Ana and San Gabriel Mountains and featured a fake mountain within its bounds. Is the California Spectacular a bit overdone and a tad artificial looking? Sure, it is. But that's what makes it a perfect fit for this land of illusion and make-believe.

ANGEL STADIUM OF ANAHEIM

- Pose for a photo beneath the **gigantic Angels batting helmets** outside the main entrance
- Visit the **statue of Gene Autry** on the first level concourse where the "Singing Cowboy" is depicted holding out his trademark cowboy hat
- Check out the **2002 World Championship Trophy** on the first level concourse

BALLPARK BUCKET LIST

68 *San Diego Padres*

THE WESTERN METAL SUPPLY COMPANY BUILDING AT PETCO PARK

When San Diego's Gaslight District was first being considered for a new Padres ballpark, most people assumed the ancient warehouse on the proposed site would be demolished. But once the ballpark designers at Populous got a look at the building conceived by revered architect Henry Lord Gay and built in 1909, they decided the opportunity to incorporate it into the ballpark blueprints was too rich to pass up. If they rotated home plate just a tad from its traditional northeast orientation toward true north, they could put the building's four floors and roof to use. And so, the firm that had similarly rehabilitated the B&O Warehouse in Baltimore got to work.

By the time Petco Park opened in 2004, it featured a refurbished outfield structure that went even a step beyond the old building at Oriole Park by abutting the playing field and offering an array of seating options. As broadcasts and highlights from San Diego showcased the Western Metal Supply Company building's multiple tiers of home-run territory viewing locations and the 10-foot-high white letters spelling out its name across its top, the once forgotten structure quickly became the defining characteristic of San Diego's new ballpark.

The building houses a clubhouse store (ground level), private suites with indoor and outdoor seating (second and third levels), and a ballpark restaurant (fourth level). And the roof houses a bank of bleachers that can also be retracted to create a general admission standing area more than 80 feet above the field.

" *Ballpark Chatter* "

"This building is the magnet for Petco Park. People are just drawn to it. It's always held that promise to become for San Diego what the warehouse is to Camden Yards, what the bleacher seats are to Wrigley Field, or the Green Monster is to Fenway Park."

—STEVE VIOLETTA, FORMER PADRES EXECUTIVE

Sailors assigned to the Carl Vinson Carrier Strike Group file onto the Petco Park lawn through a door in the Western Metal Supply Company building during a ceremony prior to a 2015 game. Another view of the porches of the Western Metal Supply Company building shows how they look when less populated.

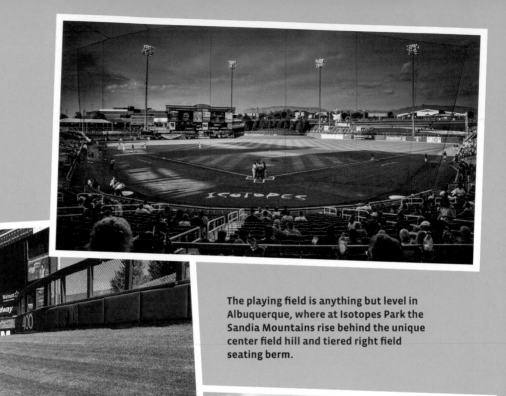

The playing field is anything but level in Albuquerque, where at Isotopes Park the Sandia Mountains rise behind the unique center field hill and tiered right field seating berm.

THE OUTFIELD SLOPE AT ISOTOPES PARK

You won't find an entry among these pages dedicated to Tal's Hill—the 4-foot-high, 90-foot-long bluff that was an original feature of Houston's Minute Maid Park when it opened in 2000. Some fans loved the center field hill, while others lamented the injury risk to which they claimed it subjected players. The hill was demolished after the 2016 season, and that leaves Isotopes Park as the only professional field with a sloped lawn like the ones once found at early twentieth century parks.

Whether you loved Tal's Hill or hated it, you had to admit its presence made flyballs in Houston more interesting than those struck elsewhere. And that is also true of the incline at Isotopes Park, where an already attractive outfield view is further enhanced by the 4.5-foot-high, 127-foot-long slope that extends from right-center to left-center. In Albuquerque's thin air, outfielders must contend with the 20-foot-wide bluff as they chase after deep flyballs.

This hill's concave shape makes it all the more distinctive. It traces a fence that is 428 feet from home plate in right- and left-center, but just 400 feet from the plate in dead center. The protruding middle of the hill makes it seem closer to the infield than it really is.

Beyond the fence, you find a right field seating berm that, unlike other berms, which offer continuous slopes of grass, provides several different tiers, each of which includes a brick seating ledge. Believe it or not, this unique seating area exists where the park once housed a "park-and-watch" section when it was known as Albuquerque Sports Stadium. If you were attending an Albuquerque Dukes game in the 1990s or early 2000s, you could pull right up to the ledge and watch the game drive-in-movie style.

Finally, beyond the outfield seating berm, the peaks of the Sandia Mountains complete the outfield view.

ISOTOPES PARK

- Gaze at the sparkling **stained glass windows** on the stadium's exterior facade
- Enjoy an **Indian Taco**, which comes on fry bread with beef, beans, and your choice of toppings
- Keep a close eye on **Orbit**, the park's goofy alien mascot

BALLPARK BUCKET LIST

ROLL CALL AT YANKEE STADIUM

After the Yankees' starting pitcher delivers the game's first pitch, the sound of clapping begins to emanate from Yankee Stadium's right field bleachers. It grows louder and louder until the Bleacher Creatures' roll call leader for the day barks out the name of the Yankees starting center fielder. Then, the other rooters in Section 203 chant the player's name until he turns and acknowledges them. Next, the barker calls out the left fielder's name, then the right fielder's, first baseman's, second baseman's, shortstop's, and third baseman's, as the ritual plays out over several pitches. Only when every starting fielder, excepting the pitcher and catcher, has acknowledged the fans do the Bleacher Creatures sit down and watch the game.

This special ballpark tradition began in the 1990s when an elderly Bronx resident named Ali Ramirez organized his fellow fans in Section 39 of the previous Yankee Stadium. Over the course of many seasons, Ramirez and the other Bleacher Creatures had built a rapport with popular Yankees like Bernie Williams, Paul O'Neill, and Tino Martinez. The Creatures were pleasantly surprised one day when their first-inning cheers for Martinez were greeted with a glove-wave. So, they called out the other starters' names and eventually got them all to offer a response.

Before long, the daily roll call had become one of the defining aspects of the Yankee Stadium experience . . . and not just for fans. Third baseman Scott Brosius would wait for nearly a minute before tipping his cap, soaking up the chants in the meantime. Johnny Damon would drop to a knee and point. Nick Swisher would offer a military salute. Curtis Granderson would take a crow-hop and wave.

Two decades after the tradition began, the roll call has been copied by Mets fans at Citi Field as well as by other teams' fans at their parks.

> ## " *Ballpark Chatter* "
>
> **"I've noticed it in other ballparks outside of Citi Field, so it's definitely spreading outside of New York . . . So it's a tribute to the Yankee fans. It's definitely something they've done and made it popular, and everybody loves it."**
>
> —CURTIS GRANDERSON, AFTER METS FANS DID THEIR OWN VERSION OF ROLL CALL AT CITI FIELD IN 2015

Former Yankee pitcher David Wells joined the Bleacher Creatures during this 2009 game. The most devoted Yankee fans sit in the right field bleachers.

Menacing tigers greet fans at Comerica Park's main entrance, colorfully adorn the scoreboard, and guard the right field entrance.

THE PROWLING TIGERS AT COMERICA PARK

Contrary to what you might have assumed, historic records offer no indication that tigers once prowled the banks of the Detroit River. Rather, baseball lore offers conflicting accounts of how the American League's oldest continuously named franchise earned its stripes.

One origin story says the Detroit Tigers were named after a particularly ferocious local militia known as the Detroit Light Guard, and nicknamed the Tigers, that fought with distinction in both the Civil War and Spanish-American War.

Another story says George Stallings, the franchise's first manager, dressed his players in orange and black striped socks during Detroit's inaugural 1901 season and the snazzy look prompted local fans to begin referring to their boys of summer as Tigers.

Yet another story proclaims that a local sportswriter, who had gone to Princeton University, compared the Detroit team to his alma mater's fighting Tigers in a game story detailing an epic comeback one day and the name caught on.

However the Tigers came by their name, when Comerica Park opened in 2000, Detroit went all out to populate its new digs with larger-than-life tigers. You find two colorful 15-foot-tall fiberglass cats atop Comerica's left field scoreboard that even have glowing eyes. As menacing as these big beasts are, the park's most amazing tigers are found above the main entrance along the first base line. There, you find a colossal concrete tiger statue guarding the ballpark's entry plaza. The big kitty opens its mouth to roar and extends a paw to swat away any fans of the Tigers' American League Central Division foes who might dare intrude. Four similarly gigantic tigers also prowl atop the stadium façade. And there are even more big concrete cats guarding the park's other entrance in right field home-run territory.

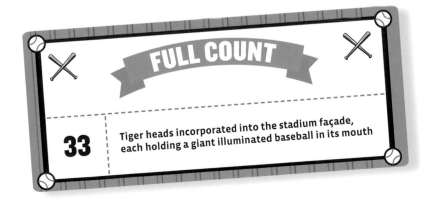

FULL COUNT

33   Tiger heads incorporated into the stadium façade, each holding a giant illuminated baseball in its mouth

THE GIANT GLOVE AT AT&T PARK

If you show up at AT&T Park early enough to watch batting practice, you just might see visiting sluggers taking aim at the *Giant 1927 Old-Time Four-Fingered Baseball Glove*. The oversized mitt sits on a pedestal in the left field stands, measuring 32 feet across. To power-hitting right-handers, it must look close enough to reach out and touch. In actuality, though, it is 501 feet from home plate. It is not a realistic target so much as a decoration when paired with the 80-foot-long Coke bottle beside it.

Created by Berkeley sculptor Ron Holthuysen, the glove is believed to be the world's largest (sorry, Iowa Cubs fans, but the inflatable mitt atop Principal Park's left field restaurant is just a big balloon). The core consists of fiberglass layered onto a steel frame, while the surface is made of a soft epoxy compound that resembles worn leather. For stitching, the artist used marine-grade rope woven through large brass rings.

The thirty-six-times-scale glove was inspired by a 1940s-era mitt Giants front office executive Jack Bair kept in his office at Candlestick Park. After that glove, which had belonged to Bair's father, gave the Giants the idea to recreate an old-time glove at their new park, the team commissioned Holthuysen. The sculptor found a circa-1927 four-fingered Rawlings glove at a nearby salvage shop, bought it for fifteen dollars, and made a 3-D model on his computer. Then, he got to work. The product of his efforts has loomed over left field at AT&T Park since its opening in 2000, casting an only-in-San-Francisco ballpark shadow.

Back in the 1920s, in case you are wondering, most players had five fingers just as they do today, but placed their pinkie fingers beside their ring fingers in their gloves' oversized fourth finger slots.

" Ballpark Chatter "

**"I am from Holland,
so I know nothing about baseball."**
—RON HOLTHUYSEN, AT&T PARK GIANT GLOVE SCULPTOR

The Coke bottle and Giant Glove loom over the left field stands.

Boog Powell signs autographs and mingles with fans at his Eutaw Street stand, and delivers a ceremonial first pitch at Oriole Park.

BOOG'S BARBECUE AT ORIOLE PARK AT CAMDEN YARDS

When the Orioles opened their beautiful new home in 1992, they served notice to the rest of the baseball world that the time had come to improve the concession offerings at America's parks. Although Oriole Park has always offered crab cakes and other regional specialties, the highlight of any trip to Camden Yards remains the scrumptious barbecued meat served with a smile by former Orioles first baseman Boog Powell.

You find Boog's Barbecue in the shadows of the B&O Warehouse on the stretch of Eutaw Street that sits within the park's bounds. As the famous pit's smoke billows into the air, you can't help but heed its scintillating siren's call. You rise from your seat like a man or woman possessed and follow the aroma of smoking meat to the area behind the right field seats.

Arriving at the stand, you find a menu featuring smoked beef, pork, and chicken, as well as turkey legs, homemade kettle chips, baked beans, coleslaw, and other southern fixings. As delicious as the food is, the chance to meet the former Orioles slugger after which the stand is named is just as enticing. Powell, who hit 339 home runs over a seventeen-year career, is happy to pose for photos and sign ticket stubs and even napkins. And he'll talk your ear off about not only baseball but proper smoking methods and which sauces go best with which meats. This is, after all, a guy who has penned two cookbooks!

Powell grew up in Lakeland, Florida, learning to cook from his mother, his grandmother, and his father, Red, who taught him to grill ribs over an open pit. During his playing days, he would often host elaborate meals for his Orioles teammates.

" *Ballpark Chatter* "

"We didn't make much money, so we all went out together. Boog was a good cook, a big fellow who enjoyed life. He would have parties at his house and barbecue for everybody."
—ANDY ETCHEBARREN, FORMER ORIOLES CATCHER AND BOOG POWELL TEAMMATE

THE PLAYER PORTRAITS AT
MCCOY STADIUM

The most elaborate tip of the cap offered by a minor-league team to its former players may be found at McCoy Stadium. The top team in the Red Sox farm system honors its alumni along its park's spiraling entrance ramps, where 3-by-6-foot portraits depict PawSox who went on to the Bigs. The gallery includes stars, as well as others who enjoyed brief careers in the Show.

Taking a mid-inning stroll to peruse the portraits prompts you to recall players you haven't thought of in years, such as flash-in-the-pan slugger Sam Horn, eccentric hurler Mark Fidrych, and goofy utility player Steve Lyons, famous for pulling down his pants after sliding into first base.

Looking at the youthful portrayals of more familiar players like Carlton Fisk, Roger Clemens, "Oil Can" Boyd, and Wade Boggs, meanwhile, reminds you of how quickly Father Time ushers all of us into the middle and then later innings of our lives.

The PawSox first began honoring players this way during the 1980s when team owner Ben Mondor commissioned a local artist to paint the likenesses of Boggs, Jim Rice, Fisk, Fred Lynn, Bruce Hurst, John Tudor, Cecil Cooper, and other PawSox favorites right on the park's stucco walls. Unfortunately, a renovation in the 1990s wiped away those 8-foot-high paintings. The team hired a different artist to create about fifty individual player canvases that were hung along the entrance ramps.

When railings were added to the ramps in the 2000s, the portraits no longer fit, and many of them were auctioned off to raise money for a local arts-education center. But the PawSox eventually recreated and rehung many of the originals in slightly smaller form.

" *Ballpark Chatter* "

**"I remember when I first started painting the murals
on the walls, it was in April, and the paint would
be freezing coming out of the can!"**

—TAYO HEUSER, ARTIST WHO PAINTED THE ORIGINAL MCCOY STADIUM MURALS

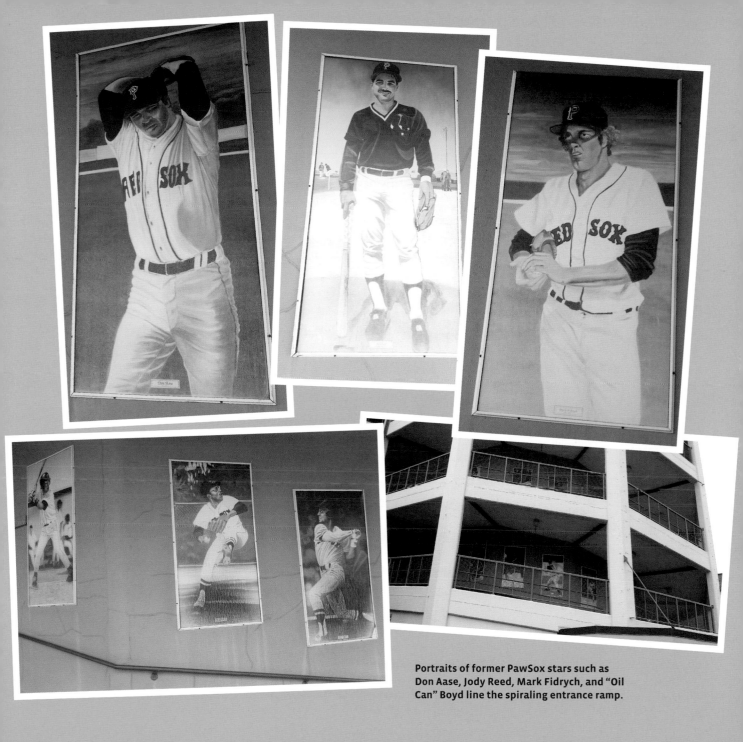

Portraits of former PawSox stars such as
Don Aase, Jody Reed, Mark Fidrych, and "Oil
Can" Boyd line the spiraling entrance ramp.

The sun shines on the Leap-the-Dips tracks during the pregame hour.

THE ROLLER COASTER AT PEOPLES NATURAL GAS FIELD

For nearly eight decades, professional baseball teams rode the rails, synthesizing in the American consciousness baseball and rail travel. The two entities remained fused until the 1950s when big-league teams took to the airways and minor-league teams to the highways. Upon visiting Altoona's Peoples Natural Gas Field today, and taking in the looming Leap-the-Dips roller coaster beyond its right field fence, you can't help but wax romantic for an earlier time.

The roller coaster's white wooden rails dominate the Altoona ballpark's outfield view, climbing 70 feet high. The coaster was built in 1902 but did not arrive at Altoona's Lakemont Park until 1987; previously, it had stood at an amusement park in Canandaigua, New York. A decade after the ride's relocation to Altoona, the city got to work building a ballpark, and since 1999 that park has treated fans to views of cars rattling along the tracks, and riders to views of the field.

In Altoona, especially, a set of tracks makes for the perfect outfield accoutrement. After all, the Curve are named after a famous stretch of tracks, known as the Horseshoe Curve, that lay in a wooded valley just west of downtown.

The nods to the region's railroading identity don't stop with the team name and outfield coaster. Continuing the theme, the exterior façade of Peoples Natural Gas Field resembles a railroad roundhouse. The semi-circular buildings were essential back in the days when trains couldn't drive in reverse, as they allowed trains to receive maintenance and then change direction.

Once inside the park, you can follow the concourse to a special row of seats atop the left field fence dubbed the Rail Kings seats. You can enjoy the antics of a crazy mascot named Loco, as in locomotive. And you can gaze all game long upon the towering roller coaster in right field.

PEOPLES NATURAL GAS FIELD

- Take a funicular ride from the **Horseshoe Curve visitor center** (2400 Veterans Memorial Highway) up to Altoona's famous set of tracks

- Visit **Lakemont Park** for a pregame ride on the **Leap-the-Dips roller coaster**

- Watch batting practice from the **Rail Kings seats** overhanging the left field warning track

BALLPARK BUCKET LIST

★ THE POLO GROUNDS' ★
CAVERNOUS CENTER FIELD, 1883–1963

The original Polo Grounds opened in 1876 as a polo stadium. It hosted its first baseball game in 1880, when the New York Metropolitans took the field, and by 1890 was the home of the Giants. When retrofitted for baseball, its fences in right and left field measured just 258 feet and 279 feet from the plate, while the fence in straightaway center was said to measure 505 feet, despite being marked at 475 and 483 feet at various times.

BUT DID THEY EVER PLAY POLO ON THESE GROUNDS?

- After a fire destroyed the third incarnation of the Polo Grounds in 1911, the Giants built the version of the park that would stand until 1964.
- In 1921 and 1922, the Polo Grounds hosted every game of the World Series, with the landlord Giants beating the tenant Yankees both times.
- Only four hitters ever cleared the Polo Grounds' center field fence: Luke Easter in 1948; Joe Adcock in 1953; Lou Brock in 1962; and Hank Aaron in 1962.

New Hampshire Fisher Cats

THE OUTFIELD HOTEL AT NORTHEAST DELTA DENTAL STADIUM

The Toronto Blue Jays' Eastern League outpost in Manchester, New Hampshire offers a special nod to the hotel windows overlooking the Blue Jays' big-league field in Toronto. Manchester's outfield hotel takes the form of a seven-story Hilton Garden Inn that includes dozens of field-facing rooms, a patio restaurant in left field home-run territory, and an outdoor hot tub shaped like home plate. The southern face of the redbrick hotel spans from left field, where its regal clock tower climbs higher than any other outfield structure, to center field, where it meets the batter's eye. Watching a game from the Northeast Delta Dental Stadium seats, you find that the hotel seals in the ballpark, enhancing its intimacy.

If you spend a night at the hotel, you can roll out of bed and eat breakfast while watching batting practice from your bedroom window, and then head downstairs for a pregame drink or a bite on the patio—keeping your glove ready for any incoming projectiles. As first pitch approaches, you can walk around the corner to the stadium gates. Leave a "Go Cats" sign or other personalizing marker in your window, and you can easily pick out your room from the ballpark seats.

The hotel patio seems like an extension of the park. During batting practice you often hear outfielders yelling "heads up" as long flyballs head toward the umbrellas and tables, and then crash down.

The home-plate-shaped hot tub recalls the baseball-bat-shaped pool snowbirds once enjoyed at the San Francisco Giants' spring training camp in Casa Grande, Arizona. Here's hoping that it inspires a bat- or glove-shaped pool to open elsewhere in baseball's bushes.

NORTHEAST DELTA DENTAL STADIUM

- Have a pregame beverage at the **Samuel Adams Bar and Grill** overlooking left field
- Check out the **manually operated scoreboard** in left
- Cheer for **"Ollie,"** a trained golden retriever, who delivers fresh balls to the home plate umpire and picks up the players' bats after they toss them aside

BALLPARK BUCKET LIST

The Fisher Cats' Shane Dawson delivers a pitch against the Portland Sea Dogs during the 2016 season. The hotel patio and adjacent Samuel Adams Bar and Grill make for ideal spots to watch the game on a summer's day.

The Ben Cheney
statue

THE BEN CHENEY STATUE AT CHENEY STADIUM

Sitting along the first base line at Cheney Stadium, you find a life-size statue depicting stadium namesake Ben Cheney, the lumber king, sports enthusiast, philanthropist, and all-around good guy who helped bring minor-league ball to Tacoma in 1960.

Cheney dreamed of one day being a professional baseball player, but, like so many of us, eventually accepted his dream would never come to pass. Instead, he opened a lumber mill and became a transcendent figure in the construction industry. Cheney's mill initially specialized in cutting railroad ties. Traditionally, after the 8-foot ties were cut, the scrap wood would be sold as firewood or discarded. Cheney's innovation was to make two-by-fours from the leftover wood. Because his two-by-fours all measured 8 feet long, this eventually established a standard ceiling height across the western United States.

Cheney and another sports enthusiast named Clay Huntington began feeling out big-league teams to see if one might consider fielding a farm club in Tacoma. The pair eventually convinced the San Francisco Giants to relocate their Triple-A affiliate from Phoenix on the condition that Tacoma build a new stadium. After Cheney promised to pay for any cost overruns, a park was built using repurposed seats and light towers from Seals Stadium, which was about to be replaced by Candlestick Park.

For the next decade, Cheney would stop by the ballpark after work and enjoy the game. On May 18, 1971, though, his heart gave out and he died at age sixty-six. His legacy lives on, however, thanks to the fine ballpark bronze sculpted by Tacoma artist Paul R. Michaels. The Cheney statue has a bag of fresh roasted peanuts in his right hand and a game program and peanut shells at his feet.

" *Ballpark Chatter* "

"He couldn't hit the curve ball."
—BRAD CHENEY, EXPLAINING WHY HIS LATE FATHER WENT INTO THE LUMBER BUSINESS

THE EXPLODING TRAIN SIGN AT FIRSTENERGY STADIUM

Sitting at FirstEnergy Stadium, you often feel the rumble of trains rolling through the ballpark parking lot outside. And, even more often, you see a steaming locomotive barreling right out of the outfield hillside toward the field. The BB&T Exploding Train Sign makes every Reading rally extra special. And, as its name might suggest, periodically it even explodes!

Unlike other celebration machines that only lurch into gear when the home team smacks a homer or clinches a win, Reading's train cranks up as soon as the Fightin Phils get a runner into scoring position. As the pressure on the opposing pitcher mounts, the sign becomes increasingly animated, helping to stoke the rally. And when the Fightins finally push a runner across the plate, it goes ballistic.

Installed at the start of the 2005 season, the sign incorporates a railroad crossing's familiar flashing lights and a train engine. The graphic served as Reading's official logo from 1999 to 2007 and, even after the club's rebranding, remains a beloved part of the Reading ballpark experience. It also recalls, of course, the Reading Railroad square on the original Monopoly game board.

Prior to each game, the public address announcer directs your attention to the board, announcing:

> Check out the BB&T Exploding Train sign located in center field. When the Fightin
> Phils have a runner in scoring position, the red lights will blink and smoke will begin
> to billow from the train's smoke stack—signaling the impending arrival of some
> Fightins' runs. Each time the Fightins score, the train will light up and appear to roll
> toward you along the tracks and fireworks will explode from the train.

Whether you are a local rooter or visitor from afar, you can't help but get caught up in the excitement every Reading rally breathes into the ballpark thanks to this special sign.

FULL COUNT

$200 Cost to buy the Reading Railroad on the Monopoly game board

The train sign, which lights up in myriad colors as the Fightin Phils mount a rally

The Maine Monster

THE MAINE MONSTER AT HADLOCK FIELD

The Red Sox Double-A affiliate offers its own take on Fenway Park's Green Monster. Ironically, the Portland Sea Dogs' Maine Monster presents a version of the big green wall that more closely resembles the structure Boston fans who came of age in the 1980s and 1990s remember than the wall at Fenway does today. While seats were added to the Red Sox wall in 2003, the Sea Dogs' wall is topped by a long horizontal net like the one that existed above the Boston landmark for decades. Likewise, the yellow numbers on the wall in Portland, announcing its distance from home plate at 315 feet, match the numbers Fenway's wall displayed prior to its being re-measured and re-marked at 310 feet in 1995. The giant Coke bottle atop the Portland wall, too, recalls the three 25-foot-tall bottles that were affixed to a Fenway light tower from 1997 through 2008.

Of course, the similarities between the two walls also abound: Both rise 37 feet; both have built-in scoreboards bearing Morse code messages; and both are green, even if Portland's wall is a slightly darker shade.

The Maine Monster has stood since 2003 when Marlins owner John Henry divested himself of the Marlins to purchase the Red Sox, and the Sea Dogs' affiliation switched as well. Upon assuming the Boston helm, one of the first things Henry did was renew his relationship with the Sea Dogs and their owner Dan Burke, relocating the Red Sox's Eastern League prospects from Trenton, New Jersey, to Portland, where Henry's Marlins minor leaguers had previously played.

Burke used his own money to replace the 8-foot-high left field wall at city-owned Hadlock Field with a Fenway tribute. Appropriately, the Morse code message on the Portland scoreboard signals the initials of Burke and his wife Bunny, recalling the cryptic dots and dashes honoring former Red Sox owners Tom and Jeanne Yawkey on the Boston scoreboard.

HADLOCK FIELD

- Check out the **old team photos** on the concourse under the third base stands to see what memorable Marlins and Red Sox stars looked like when they were just kids

- Stuff your hot dog wrappers and french fry containers into the belly of the nearest **trash monster** as the goofy mascots amble through the stands

- Cheer for the pine tree, blueberry, lobster, or potato during the midgame running of the **Maine Race**

BALLPARK BUCKET LIST

THE BUCK O'NEIL LEGACY SEAT AT KAUFFMAN STADIUM

Former Kansas City Monarchs star Buck O'Neil would have surely delivered one of the great Hall of Fame induction speeches of all time. But he was not chosen. Fortunately, though, a year after Cooperstown's 2006 special election to admit Negro Leagues stars snubbed O'Neil, the Royals unveiled an innovative tribute at Kauffman Stadium to honor the gentleman Ken Burns's 1994 documentary, *Baseball*, made famous: a special seat behind home plate and accompanying program named in O'Neil's memory.

Even before Burns found him, O'Neil and some of his fellow Negro Leagues alumni had pooled their mementos and resources to open a small museum in downtown Kansas City. After the PBS miniseries shined a light on the Negro Leagues' fascinating stories of perseverance and friendship, the city of Kansas City relocated and expanded the Negro Leagues Baseball Museum in 1997.

Fittingly, the Royals' Buck O'Neil Legacy Seat Program welcomes a different person to Kauffman Stadium each day to enjoy a game from the seat. The program honors Kansas Citians whose lives reflect the generosity of spirit that guided O'Neil. Over the course of a typical Royals homestand, the seat might welcome a teacher of children with special needs, a teen who volunteers at a local senior center, an inner-city baseball coach, and an eight-year-old who has been collecting canned goods for a food bank. Each honoree is acknowledged in a pregame ceremony and thanked during the game via a P.A. announcement.

The Buck O'Neil Legacy Seat is in Section 127, Row C, behind home plate. As game-time approaches, the ushers usually guard the lower boxes tightly, so be sure to check out the seat shortly after the ballpark gates open. Then, applaud the O'Neil Seat's occupant when his or her name is announced.

 Ballpark Chatter

"Waste no tears for me.
I didn't come along too early.
I was right on time."

—BUCK O'NEIL

The Buck O'Neil Legacy Seat is the lone red seat at
Kauffman Stadium.

The train shed gives the right side of the infield a distinctive character.

THE TRAIN SHED AT MONTGOMERY RIVERWALK STADIUM

As the unveiling of Oriole Park at Camden Yards inspired the ballpark renaissance of the 1990s and 2000s, big-league cities across the United States sought to incorporate into their stadiums venerable edifices that had once stood proudly in their cities before falling into disrepair. One minor-league city also went all in when it came to merging its civic past with its baseball present: Montgomery, Alabama. The city opened a new park in the heart of downtown in 2004 that incorporates a railroad storage facility that has stood in its present location since 1898. The ancient train shed both enhances the Montgomery Riverwalk Stadium atmosphere and offers unique seating and dining options for fans along the first base line.

From streets outside the park, the train shed projects an old-time look that blends in nicely with the other structures in the old railroad district. You could pass by it and hardly realize a professional ball field lies inside. After you buy your ticket from a window built right into the train shed and pass through its main entrance, there is little doubt, though, that you have arrived at a ballpark, and an absolutely beautiful one at that.

As the game progresses, you can visit the Railyard concession stand or Club Car Bar, which are also built right into the old shed at ground level. On the shed's second level, meanwhile, you find six luxury suites offering high rollers a bird's-eye view of the game.

Whether or not you are lucky enough to find your way into the upstairs seats, a trip to Montgomery treats you to a ballpark experience made all the more charming by its nineteenth-century train shed. With its arched doorways and off-white façade, it creates a warm, cozy feeling at an urban park just two blocks away from a still-functioning train station.

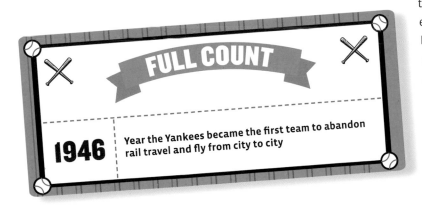

FULL COUNT

1946 Year the Yankees became the first team to abandon rail travel and fly from city to city

82 *Miami Marlins*

THE HOME RUN SCULPTURE AT MARLINS PARK

No Marlins Park attraction symbolizes the park's departure from the retro-classic design sensibility that characterized the new ballparks of the 1990s and 2000s better than the colorful Home Run Sculpture located beyond its left-center field fence.

With its leaping marlins, pink flamingos, flying seabirds, palm trees, bright yellow sun, and eruptions of spewing seawater, the gaudy celebration machine fits perfectly in a city that lights its skyline in glowing pastels at night and inspires the edgiest of fashion designers to be even edgier.

Alternately referred to as the "Home Run Feature" or "Home Run Display," the Home Run Sculpture was created by legendary pop artist Red Grooms, who is a friend of Jeffrey Loria, the Marlins owner who made his fortune as an art dealer.

Shortly after the Marlins' new home opened in 2012, the sculpture began drawing criticism. Some people lamented Marlins Park's use of public funding, calling the sculpture's $2.5 million price tag outrageous. Others objected to the sculpture on aesthetic grounds, calling it gaudy, psychedelic, and disgusting, and those are only the adjectives we can print in a family publication. Even some opposing players chimed in, claiming the sculpture was a distraction to them as they dug into the batter's box.

Even if you enter Marlins Park as a skeptic, you may find yourself warming to the Home Run Sculpture as you get your bearings within the futuristic baseball grounds to which it belongs. You have to admit, the 76-foot-tall screaming heap of swirling color gives you reason to root with extra gusto for a Giancarlo Stanton long ball. It is a little zany but is a sight to behold, much like Miami itself.

" *Ballpark Chatter* "

"All those descriptions of gaudy, or extremely colorful, actually do apply to the majority of my work. So as far as that's concerned, it's par for the course. But in this situation, people that aren't really in the know about art very much are seeing it very fresh."

—RED GROOMS, CREATOR OF THE HOME RUN SCULPTURE

The Home Run Sculpture,
which lights up to celebrate
a Marlins home run

An iron man behind the plate, Carlton Fisk now stands rendered in bronze while Harold Baines waits for the pitch.

THE STATUES AT U.S. CELLULAR FIELD

For a team that began 2017 having won a single world championship over the past century, the Chicago White Sox sure have had a lot of iconic players, and their ballpark does a nice job honoring them in bronze. The legends of every White Sox era stand on the U.S. Cellular Field first-level concourse overlooking the outfield.

The first statue was installed in 2003 on the right-center field concourse to honor team founder Charles Comiskey. "The Old Roman" is depicted wearing a derby hat and bowtie as he leans on a bat.

In 2004, the White Sox added a bronze of Minnie Minoso on the other side of the batter's eye. Minoso played parts of five decades in the big leagues, getting his first taste of the Bigs with the Indians in 1949 and spanning the decades until tallying two at-bats with the White Sox in 1980 as a Bill Veeck promotional stunt. Over the next several seasons, the White Sox added a statue or two each year, usually at midseason ceremonies involving the subject and/or his surviving family members.

Carlton Fisk, standing proudly in his colorful shin guards and chest protector, joined the assembly in 2005. The keystone combination of Nellie Fox and Luis Aparicio arrived in 2006.

Billy Pierce, rearing back to deliver a pitch, joined the crew in 2007, followed by Harold Baines in 2008, Frank Thomas in 2011, and Paul Konerko in 2014. Thomas watches a clout sure to touch down somewhere in the bleachers, while Konerko raises a fist in celebration, as he did after smacking a clutch grand slam in the 2005 World Series.

The White Sox' collection makes for a fun stroll through team history. Just don't expect to find a Joe Jackson statue at U.S. Cellular Field, as apparently Major League Baseball's ban of "Shoeless Joe" extends even to likenesses in bronze.

" *Ballpark Chatter* "

"I love it.
They even got my nose right."

—FRANK THOMAS

84 *Pulaski Yankees*

THE STONE CASTLE AT CALFEE PARK

Set amid the rolling green hills of the Blue Ridge Mountain Range in a tiny southwestern Virginia town, you find an Appalachian League ballpark that offers as homey an experience as you will find at the professional level. Arriving at Calfee Park, you encounter its signature feature before you even lay eyes on the field. Well, you encounter it if you opt to enter the park through its left field entrance, rather than the one behind home plate. With its gray stones and gates made of wrought iron, this original entrance to the park resembles an ancient English castle. Upon passing through the castle's arched doorways, you arrive at a walkway that leads down the left field line toward the grandstand.

Built in 1935 as part of President Franklin Delano Roosevelt's Works Progress Administration, Calfee Park has been renovated through the years—most recently during the winters of 2014 and 2015—but still offers only about 2,500 seats and feels as cozy as a pro park can be.

The home plate entrance is designated for those holding Reserved tickets, while the left field gate is the entrance for General Admission ticket holders. Even if you plan to sit in one of the numbered seats, though, you should enter through the historic left field gate to have the full Calfee Park experience. As you file through, notice the year of the park's construction etched in stone overhead, as well as the park's original name—Pulaski Athletic Field.

Once inside, you see that the residential neighborhood you drove and walked through to reach the park enhances the ballpark atmosphere. Beyond the fence in right field, you find several homes whose occupants can sit in their backyards to enjoy free baseball from the hillside overlooking the field.

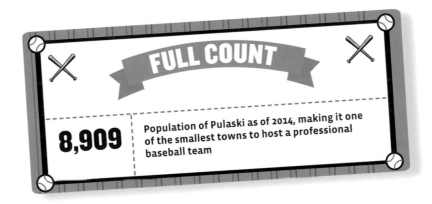

FULL COUNT

8,909 Population of Pulaski as of 2014, making it one of the smallest towns to host a professional baseball team

The Calfee Park
entrance

At Bosse Field, fans are encouraged to "Support the Racine Belles," even if the Belles never played at the park.

THE RACINE BELLES SIGNS AT BOSSE FIELD

A journey to Evansville, Indiana, offers you the chance to explore one of the primary film sites for the 1992 baseball movie *A League of Their Own*. After the Columbia Pictures trailers rolled out of the Bosse Field parking lot, the locals left intact the period-specific advertisements and signage installed throughout the park for the movie. And today you find these interesting mementos adorning the grandstand and tunnels that run from the stands to the concourse. The vintage directional signs point you toward the bathrooms and concession stands, while large ads implore you to "Support the Racine Belles."

The movie provides a fictional account of the All-American Girls Professional Baseball League (AAG-PBL), which rose to prominence in the 1940s while many of America's men were fighting World War II. The major leagues continued play during the war, even as many stars left to fight in foreign theaters, but a great number of bush-league teams ceased operations. That left a void in small towns across America, which led visionaries Philip K. Wrigley and Branch Rickey to launch the AAGPBL.

Half a century later, when Columbia Pictures set out to make a film chronicling the plight of the Rockford Peaches, Bosse Field—which still bore the vintage look of the 1940s—was cast as the home of the Racine Belles. Evansville was actually without a minor-league team at the time, which made filming possible during the hot summer months of 1991. Locals even served as extras, dressing in old-fashioned woolen hats and coats and sitting in the sweltering Bosse Field stands while Tom Hanks, Madonna, Rosie O'Donnell, and Geena Davis filmed take after take on the field.

In actuality, there never was an AAGPBL team in Evansville, although Indiana cities like South Bend and Fort Wayne did field teams. The real-life Belles played at Horlick Field in Racine, Wisconsin.

" *Ballpark Chatter* "

"If you want to go back to Oregon and make a hundred babies, great . . . But sneaking out like this, quitting, you'll regret it for the rest of your life. Baseball is what gets inside you. It's what lights you up, you can't deny that."

—ROCKFORD PEACHES MANAGER JIMMY DUGAN, PLAYED BY TOM HANKS

THE BOARDWALK AT CHARLOTTE SPORTS PARK

When a heavily renovated Charlotte Sports Park opened in 2009, it introduced a whole new type of outfield viewing area—a 19,000-square-foot "Baseball Boardwalk" that runs atop the outfield fence. The festive deck offers a space where you can stand and watch the game while mingling with friends. From the boardwalk's planks, you can also look down into the bullpens, scramble after home-run balls, and purchase frosty beverages from the park's left field tiki bar.

While standing for nine innings may not sound appealing, you should give the experience a try for at least a few innings to enjoy the game in a new way. A General Admission ticket allows you to sit on the berm in right field foul territory, to sit on the berm that wraps around the left field foul pole, or to stand on the boardwalk, so you can use this low-cost option to sample a few different vantage points.

Here's betting your time on the boardwalk will be what you remember most after heading home. You can sit in an infield seat at any old ballpark, and on a berm at many minor-league parks, but where else can you watch a game from a boardwalk overlooking the outfield?

Interestingly, this ballpark novelty was created more by necessity than inspired design. Initially Charlotte County—which footed the largest share of the ballpark's $27 million renovation—had hoped to add a large berm across the outfield. But environmental concerns related to two ponds beyond the left field fence derailed that plan. Undeterred, the designers at Populous created instead a deck that could hug the outfield footprint more tightly than a seating lawn could. And today, Charlotte's Baseball Boardwalk provides a one-of-a-kind viewing experience, while giving Charlotte Sports Park its most distinctive characteristic.

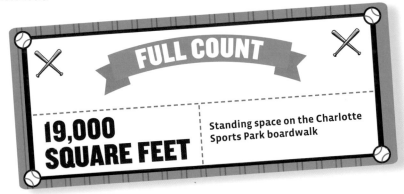

FULL COUNT

19,000 SQUARE FEET Standing space on the Charlotte Sports Park boardwalk

Fans line the boardwalk—which begins by the right field foul pole—during Rays' spring training games at the home of the Charlotte Stone Crabs.

Fans watch the game from Levi's Landing with the waters of McCovey Cove at their back. Meanwhile, the Splash Hit Counter remained stuck on 68 throughout the entire 2015 season.

LEVI'S LANDING AT AT&T PARK

The 24-foot-tall brick wall that separates AT&T Park from McCovey Cove honors Giants legend Willie Mays, who wore No. 24 as a member of the New York and then San Francisco Giants. The unusually shaped right field parcel the wall creates, meanwhile, recalls the right field dimensions at the Polo Grounds. Down the right field line, the waters of McCovey Cove seem eminently reachable to left-handed pull hitters, but the wall slants quickly away from home plate. After teasing sluggers with a posted distance of 309 feet down the line, the wall torments them with a distance of 421 feet to right-center.

The wall—formally known as Levi's Landing, thanks to a sponsorship deal with one of San Francisco's most iconic clothiers—is no mere frill. If not for some sort of towering edifice along the water's edge, it would not have been possible for San Francisco to squeeze a ballpark into this cozy plot on the shores of Mission Creek. So we can thank the wall for making the terrific water views possible, as well as for creating the right field pasture.

While fans throughout the park enjoy these features, three rows of lucky fans have the pleasure of sitting atop the wall in arcade-style seating. Behind them, four brick pillars shoot water into the air whenever a Giants player hits a home run.

The wall also tallies Giants homers that reach McCovey Cove with its Splash Hit Counter, which reflects the total homers the Giants have hit into the drink since the park's opening in 2000. The number stood at 68 at the close of the 2014 season . . . and at the close of the 2015 season, too, after the Giants endured their first splash hit shutout. Brandon Belt finally ended the team's drought on June 8, 2016 with a blast off Boston's David Price.

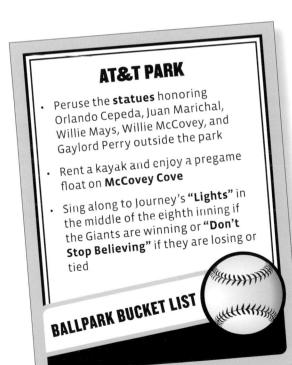

AT&T PARK

- Peruse the **statues** honoring Orlando Cepeda, Juan Marichal, Willie Mays, Willie McCovey, and Gaylord Perry outside the park

- Rent a kayak and enjoy a pregame float on **McCovey Cove**

- Sing along to Journey's **"Lights"** in the middle of the eighth inning if the Giants are winning or **"Don't Stop Believing"** if they are losing or tied

BALLPARK BUCKET LIST

★ ELYSIAN FIELDS, HOBOKEN, ★ NEW JERSEY, OCTOBER 1859

Historians agree that baseball evolved out of English precursors like cricket throughout the 1800s, and that there is no one primordial field where it may be said the "first" baseball game took place. Hoboken, New Jersey's Elysian Fields is, however, considered the site where Alexander Joy Cartwright and his New York Knickerbocker teammates drafted the first written set of rules for a game resembling baseball as we know it today.

ON THE BIRTH OF BASEBALL

- For years, Cooperstown, New York's Doubleday Field was considered the site where the first baseball game was played on the basis of sports-equipment magnate Albert Spalding's Mills Commission declaring it the birthplace of baseball in 1907.

- The first documented game at Elysian Fields took place June 19, 1846, with the Knickerbockers losing to the New York Nine, 23–1.

- The Elysian diamond is commemorated today in Hoboken by four bronze bases laid in concrete at the corners of the intersection of 11th and Washington.

THE AMERICAN NATIONAL GAME OF BASE BALL.

GRAND MATCH FOR THE CHAMPIONSHIP AT THE ELYSIAN FIELDS, HOBOKEN, N.J.

88 Salem Red Sox

MINI FENWAY AT LEWIS-GALE FIELD AT SALEM MEMORIAL BASEBALL STADIUM

Salem Memorial Baseball Stadium opened in 1995 to serve as home to the Salem Avalanche, a Carolina League franchise affiliated with the Colorado Rockies. After the Rockies broke ties with the club in 2002, the Avalanche signed a player development contract with the Houston Astros that ran through 2008. In the dying days of that affiliation, the team was purchased by the Fenway Sports Group, a subsidiary of the Boston Red Sox. And thus began the story of how there came to be a miniature Green Monster, complete with a Fenway-style scoreboard, in Salem, Virginia.

After the Salem club became part of the Red Sox chain in 2009, it changed its name to "Salem Red Sox" and to further cement its bond with its big-league parent, began work with the city of Salem, which owns the ballpark, on "Mini Fenway." The elaborate Wiffle Ball diamond lies between the third base grandstand and the brick building that houses the Salem-Roanoke Baseball Hall of Fame. It is accessible to ticket holders on game day.

For rambunctious kids who just can't sit still for nine innings, or older fans who have always dreamed of taking a few swings at the most famous wall in sports, the replica field is a wonderful attraction. Mini Fenway allows you to play a version of the game you have come to watch, while it simultaneously channels the spirit of the big-league yard the pros on the abutting field are hoping to one day reach.

After the Scotts Company installed its lawn, Mini Fenway opened in June 2010. It has been a hit ever since. What does it feel like to loft a flyball over Fenway's famous left field wall? Dig into the batter's box in Salem and take a swing for the fences to find out!

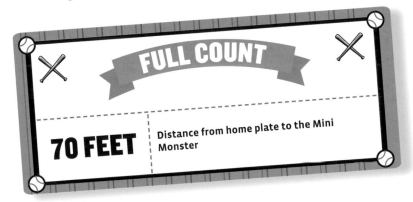

FULL COUNT

70 FEET — Distance from home plate to the Mini Monster

Young fans play ball in the shadow of Salem's faux Green Monster, the scoreboard of which mimics Fenway Park's slate board.

Young fans cool off in the Principal Park fountain.

THE WATER FOUNTAIN AT PRINCIPAL PARK

Saying it gets hot in central Iowa during the summer months is like saying the folks in these parts kind of like the Cubs. Both are glaring understatements. Thankfully, the Iowa Cubs go to considerable lengths to ensure your safety and comfort at steamy Principal Park. In a refreshing departure from ballparks' usually profiteering ways, the team offers free sunscreen and ice water on the ballpark concourse. It is the park's prominent right field water fountain, though, that makes the Des Moines baseball experience truly distinctive. Set above the right field fence, the fountain not only looks pretty but cools you down on game day.

Upon passing through Principal Park's right field entrance, you encounter the fountain almost immediately, taking the form of a single pillar rising from a patio sculpted to look like a giant baseball. The pillar shoots water high into the air throughout the game and a little higher when the Iowa Cubs have a home run to celebrate. In addition to the water spraying from this 8-foot-high center structure, water shoots from jets set within the patio ball's faux stitching.

The best thing about the fountain, perhaps, is its accessibility. At any point in the game, you are free to head to right field to cool off.

If the idea of cooling off in a fountain sounds pleasing enough to you, but spending the remainder of the game in wet clothes does not, then plan to wear a bathing suit to Principal Park, or bring one to change into in the men's or women's room in the middle of the game.

You haven't had the full Principal Park experience unless you have gotten a little wet, or better yet, utterly soaked. Just be sure to entrust your scorebook to someone with drier hands than you!

PRINCIPAL PARK

- Check out the **giant inflatable glove** in left field home-run territory
- Gaze upon the **golden dome** of the **Iowa State Capitol building** beyond the fence in center
- Order a locally made brew from the **Iowa Craft Beer stand** on the concourse

BALLPARK BUCKET LIST

90 Traverse City Beach Bums

THE BEACH HOUSE FAÇADE AT WUERFEL PARK

The northwest Michigan resort town of Traverse City provides the opportunity to visit one of the independent leagues' most distinctive parks. So unconventional is this facility, in fact, that upon arriving at the home of the Frontier League's Traverse City Beach Bums, you may find yourself thumbing the back arrow on your GPS, trying to determine which turn you missed along the way. The park's exterior façade looks more like a stretch of beach houses than a professional ballpark. And the structure lining the back of the grandstand inside does too. The unusual design was inspired by the similar structures found lining the nearby shores of Lake Michigan.

Pulling into the ballpark parking lot, the first thing you encounter is a tiny shack like the kind in which beach attendants sit collecting parking money. You continue along the driveway until you reach the unusual façade with its conjoined blue and white beach "houses." The windows, roofs, and porches all contribute to the illusion that you have indeed just arrived at the lakefront for a little R & R.

Inside, the luxury boxes above the concourse offer porches that look like they should be overlooking water vistas, not field views. Helping to complete the theme, comfy patio chairs line the top of the seating bowl selling as VIP Seats, while whole swaths of patio chairs and tables at the outfield ends of the seating bowl await fans who are just a little too laid back to sit in stadium seats.

Further playing on the beach motif, resident mascots Sunburn and Suntan—two bears in Beach Bums gear—provide an object lesson on why you should apply plenty of sunscreen: Sunburn is bright red and not nearly as jovial or popular as his sunglasses-wearing partner, Suntan.

" Ballpark Chatter "

"It's probably one of the highlights of my life . . ."
—BEACH BUMS OWNER JOHN WUERFEL,
AFTER THE TEAM WON THE 2015 FRONTIER LEAGUE CHAMPIONSHIP

The façade at Wuerfel Park resembles a row of beach houses.

Fans visit Aisle 4, Row 8, Seat 113 to confront an infamous moment in Cubs history.

THE BARTMAN SEAT AT WRIGLEY FIELD

Chicago's usually "Friendly Confines" became the site of a rather ugly scene during the 2003 National League Championship Series. If you are old enough to have watched Game Six, then you remember the play that provoked 40,000 diehards to turn on one of their own. Twenty-six-year-old Steve Bartman sat along the left field foul line, watching what he and countless others hoped would be the series clincher for the Cubs against the Marlins. Stealing glimpses at the field from beneath his Cubs hat and old-school headphones, Bartman watched Chicago's loveable losers carry a 3–0 lead into the eighth inning. With the Cubs ahead three games to two and starter Mark Prior cruising, they seemed poised to return to the World Series for the first time since 1945. And then, with one out and a runner on second base, the Marlins' Luis Castillo lofted a pop foul down the left field line.

Bartman stood and reached for the ball. Whether he reached out over the field remains a matter of debate, but Cubs left fielder Moises Alou thought he did. After the ball bounced off Bartman's hands and disappeared, Alou slammed his hand into his glove and unleashed a string of expletives.

Bartman sank into his seat. Left field umpire Mike Everitt ruled that the ball was in the stands and refused to call fan interference. Castillo walked. And the Marlins went on to score eight runs in the inning.

Before long, Bartman had to be escorted from Wrigley Field under police protection. The next day, his face was plastered on newspapers across the country. When the Marlins won Game Seven, he officially descended into baseball's shrine of infamy. Was it his fault the Cubs lost? No, but he took the blame.

Today, Wrigley pilgrims visit Section 4, Row 8, Seat 113 to reflect on that defining moment in Cubs' history.

" *Ballpark Chatter* "

"I am so truly sorry from the bottom of this Cubs fan's broken heart."

—STEVE BARTMAN, IN A STATEMENT RELEASED SHORTLY AFTER THE "BARTMAN INCIDENT"

THE ZIZ AT GOODYEAR BALLPARK

Approaching the spring home of the Cincinnati Reds and Cleveland Indians, your eyes are drawn to a distinctive piece of art known as *The Ziz*, the white surface of which gleams in the sunshine, the red seams of which reach ever skyward. It must be a ball, you think, but it isn't shaped like any ball you have ever seen.

When you think about it, this abstract portrayal of the old horsehide seems apropos, given its placement outside a miniature park where snowbirds enjoy a version of the game that doesn't quite match the one they follow in the summertime. In Arizona's warm March air, starting pitchers usually max out at three or four innings, batting orders become larded with minor leaguers as games reach the not-so-crucial later innings, teams often call it a tie rather than play extras, and *The Ziz* stretches your conception of what a ball can be.

The sculpture reaches 60-feet, 6-inches high, mirroring the distance between home plate and the pitching rubber. Is it portraying the blur of a ball in motion, or the cover of a ball that has been cut open and gutted? It's up to you to make of *The Ziz* what you will.

Sculptor Donald Lipski has said the piece was inspired by Romanian sculptor Constantin Brancusi's "Bird in Space" series, which includes twenty narrow bronze and marble works portraying the motion of birds in flight, sans wings, feet, and beaks. Lipski created *The Ziz* from fiberglass in 2008 and 2009, working under the commission of the city of Goodyear. When finished, he named the piece after a mythic Hebrew water bird that watched over smaller birds, then attended a grand opening party where the piece was unveiled outside Goodyear Ballpark's home plate gate.

GOODYEAR BALLPARK

- Visit the home plate concourse to see the **Ohio Cup**—a 3-foot-high trophy awarded each year to the winner of the Reds and Indians' six-game regular season series
- Laugh along with **house mascot Zizzy**, whose oblong head is modeled after *The Ziz*
- Bone up on your Cactus League history by perusing the **concourse's colorful plaques** detailing Arizona baseball's seminal moments

BALLPARK BUCKET LIST

Inspired by Constantin Brancusi's "Bird in Space" series, *The Ziz* welcomes fans to Goodyear Ballpark.

The unique
left field curve
at Ashford
University Field

THE LEFT FIELD CURVE AT ASHFORD UNIVERSITY FIELD

Only a few hundred feet from the Mighty Mississippi, Ashford University Field offers a quaint covered grandstand that recalls the minor-league yards of yesteryear. But the ballpark's signature feature is its distinctive left field curve that leaves it with a unique lawn and wrap-around seating berm.

The oddly contoured left field was created during a 2005 renovation that redrew the course of the outfield fence and created a grassy seating area along it. Families sit and play on the curve, while young men and women chat, sip beverages, and otherwise hang out along the yellow home-run marker atop the chain link fence atop the wall. Because the wall and field curve so dramatically, there is more standing room along the wall top than there would be otherwise.

After looping out to left field's deepest point just after crossing into fair territory, the wall dips back toward shortstop and makes a bubble before eventually resuming a more traditional course toward center. The effect is a little bit like the bubble in right field at Banner Island Ballpark in Stockton, California, but there you find a private seating porch on the protruding parcel instead of the welcoming patch of lawn that picnickers and ball hawks enjoy in Clinton.

As you might imagine, more than just creating an exceptional viewing location for fans, Ashford University Field's left field curve also affects the happenings on the field. Deep flyballs to left field present outfielders with a greater challenge than they do at most parks. Many a visiting left fielder has staggered toward the wall with trepidation in his gait for fear of crashing into it. And so too, deep flyballs sometimes carom off the wall at unexpected angles, turning doubles into triples. Whether you are a player or a fan, the curve gives Clinton's ballpark a character all its own.

FULL COUNT

1937 Year the stadium first opened as "Riverview Stadium," to serve as home to the Clinton Owls in the old Three-I League

94 *Cleveland Indians*

#TRIBELIVE AT PROGRESSIVE FIELD

Once upon a time, we watched passively as the storylines surrounding our favorite teams unfurled. Excepting special occasions when we traveled to the ballpark, we remained consumers of game experiences rather than active participants in them. The players played and we observed. Sure, you could yell at the tube or call the local sports radio show the next day if the manager left a struggling pitcher in the game too long, but there was no way to share your thoughts more broadly in real time. All that changed, of course, with the advent of social media.

While all thirty big-league baseball teams have benefited from this online fan engagement, the Cleveland Indians have been at the forefront of embracing baseball's social media revolution. As a small-market team, it behooves the Indians to be ... umm ... progressive ... and they sure have been.

One product of Cleveland's forward-thinking is the #TribeLive seating area located beside the right field foul pole at Progressive Field. To sit in this coveted locale, you must fill out an application establishing your social media bona fides and listing some possible dates when you could attend a game. If the Indians' review of your social media accounts earns you an invitation, you receive a complimentary ticket to sit among some of the Tribe's other hyper-social fans, as well as access to a social media room within Progressive Field's right field bar, and the ability to broadcast your tweets and posts to the more than 300,000 followers of the Indians' social media channels during the game you attend.

To learn more, search for #TribeLive on your favorite social channel sometime when an Indians game is in progress and enjoy a game through the posts of those fans presently enjoying the Indians' social experience.

PROGRESSIVE FIELD

- Browse the **statues** of Indians greats Larry Doby, Bob Feller, and Jim Thome outside the park
- Visit **Heritage Park**, beyond the fence in center field, which houses the **Indians Hall of Fame** and includes a plaque honoring Ray Chapman, an Indians shortstop who died after being struck by a pitch in 1920
- Find the **retired No. 455** that honors Indians fans for helping the team sell out 455 straight games between June 12, 1995, and April 4, 2001

BALLPARK BUCKET LIST

The view from the #TribeLive seats on Opening Day 2016

The original ballpark biscuit

THE BISCUITS AT MONTGOMERY RIVERWALK STADIUM

Every so often regional primacy and marketing inspiration converge to create a ballpark treat so novel, scrumptious, and utterly original that we must imbibe in its pleasures whenever we wander into its domain. Such is the case with the ballpark biscuit at Montgomery Riverwalk Stadium. If you come from the old-school of fan tradition—the one that says, "Give me a bag of nuts, a cup of suds, a hot dog, and a box of Cracker Jack and that's all I need, bub,"—that's okay. But before you turn up your nose at this buttery ballpark concoction, you should give it a try. After all, you can fill your belly with cased meat and salty nuts at any park, but there's only one ball field where you can sample an array of different biscuit-based treats.

While in most corners of America, the biscuit is a mere afterthought, in Sweet Home Alabama the locals eschew the English muffins, breads, bagels, sandwich rounds, wraps, and ... yes ... even croissants carb-lovers go gaga over elsewhere. Here the biscuit is king.

Montgomery's Southern League team honors this regional preference with its very name, which was chosen from more than 4,000 entrees in a name-the-team contest before the Biscuits' 2004 debut. And when you name your team after a food, you had better serve it at your park and it had better be good.

Visiting the biscuit stand behind home plate, you can order your biscuit plain, and add butter, jam, or other toppings, or you can order a biscuit smothered in gravy, sweet strawberries and cream, or Alaga cane syrup, which they have been making in Montgomery since 1906.

Whether you cheer "batter up" or "butter up," you are sure to enjoy this flaky ballpark treat.

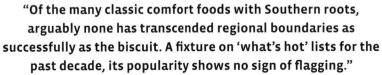

" *Ballpark Chatter* "

"Of the many classic comfort foods with Southern roots, arguably none has transcended regional boundaries as successfully as the biscuit. A fixture on 'what's hot' lists for the past decade, its popularity shows no sign of flagging."

—NANCY KRUSE, MENU TRENDS ANALYST, *NATION'S RESTAURANT NEWS*

96 El Paso Chihuahuas

THE RIGHT FIELD TOWERS AT SOUTHWEST UNIVERSITY PARK

When the Texas League's El Paso Diablos left town for a new park in Springfield, Missouri, in 2005, El Paso assumed the unenviable distinction of being the largest US city without a professional baseball team. In the years to follow, the city fielded a team in the unaffiliated American Association of Independent Professional Baseball, but the step down to indy ball didn't sit well with residents of the proud border city. And so, after a decade in baseball purgatory, El Paso got back into the affiliated game in 2014 when it opened beautiful Southwest University Park and welcomed a Pacific Coast League franchise.

The new yard was wedged into a downtown lot just big enough to host Triple-A ball. After demolishing some buildings and converting a couple of streets into pedestrian walkways, the designers had a 5-acre canvas on which to paint. On it, they created a park with different seating clusters all around the field. The most distinctive of these intimate viewing areas are the ones housed within two brick towers overlooking right field.

The three-story Santa Fe Pavilion stands in straightaway right, while the four-story Big Dog House stands closer to the foul line. A third-level pedestrian bridge connects the two. Entering the park, you follow a walkway between them to the concourse. After reaching your seat, you find the towers joining with the attractive buildings of downtown and El Paso's landmark "Star on the Mountain" to create an eclectic outfield view.

Clearly, these buildings were created with the fans in mind, first, and the players, second. The Santa Fe Pavilion offers two stories of viewing space through its open design, and the Big Dog House features a rooftop viewing deck and two floors of group seating. The visiting relievers enjoy no view of the sky, though, from their bullpen tucked below the Santa Fe Pavilion.

SOUTHWEST UNIVERSITY PARK

- Find the **Not Whole Fence sculpture** on Santa Fe Street, which offers knotholes through which you can enjoy a free view of the field
- Check out the **visitors' bullpen** tucked beneath the Santa Fe Pavilion, which offers relievers nary a view of the sky
- Stand beneath the glowing **"Star on the Ceiling"** in the clubhouse store—a nod to El Paso's famous "Star on the Mountain"

BALLPARK BUCKET LIST

The right field towers of Southwest University Park provide the backdrop to the National Anthem.

The H lights up when a play is scored a hit, and the E lights up when a play is ruled an error.

THE SUN SIGN AT ORIOLE PARK AT CAMDEN YARDS

Although we fans lament the intrusion of advertising into our green cathedrals, we should remember that ballparks have housed ads since the game's earliest days. And sometimes ballpark signs actually enhance the game-day experience. Such is the case with the Citgo sign over Fenway Park's famous Green Monster, and such was the case with the Hit Sign, Win Suit sign at Ebbets Field that promised new threads to players who dinged the outfield sign from Abe Stark's Brooklyn clothing store.

Another iconic Ebbets ad was the Schaefer Beer sign atop the scoreboard. When suspect fielding plays necessitated the official scorer render a ruling, the H in Schaefer would light up if he ruled a hit or the E if he ruled an error. From an advertising perspective, the sign was genius. After dicey plays, 30,000 people locked eyes on Schaefer while awaiting a determination. Whether those moments of suspenseful contemplation prompted fans to head to the Ebbets beer stands is anyone's guess.

Today, the most prominent descendant of the Schaefer sign stands at Oriole Park at Camden Yards. High above the right-center field scoreboard, a *Baltimore Sun* ad offers oversized orange letters that spell The Sun. As you might have guessed, the H in The lights up when the official scorer deems a play a hit, and the E when the scorer rules an error. This nod to one of the game's classic signs contributes to the old-time vibe Oriole Park creates.

So, root for a sloppily fielded game when you visit Baltimore, and you may well see the sign in action for yourself. And if you find yourself digging into your pockets for change to buy a copy of the *Baltimore Sun* from a newspaper box after the game, you will know why.

" *Ballpark Chatter* "

"The three most important things that have happened in baseball since the Second World War were Jackie Robinson taking the field in Brooklyn in 1947, free agency arriving in 1975, and Oriole Park at Camden Yards opening in 1992.

—AUTHOR GEORGE WILL, *A NICE LITTLE PLACE ON THE NORTH SIDE*

THE OUTFIELD FIRE PITS AT DOW DIAMOND

In April, the average daily low temperature is 36 degrees Fahrenheit in Midland, Michigan, and it isn't exactly balmy in May, June, July, or August. Wisely, then, years before the Minnesota Twins and Cleveland Indians would unveil fireplaces at their parks, the Great Lakes Loons introduced Midwest League fans to a new kind of gathering place in 2007: the ballpark hotspot. Actually, Dow Diamond has three of them: two outfield fire pits and a fireplace on the home plate concourse. On those frosty nights when the wind is blowing off Lake Huron, the flames sure are appreciated.

The fire pits are at the back of the right and left field seating lawns, raised so the heat hits you right where you need it the most, on the face and hands. Surrounded by 3-foot-high screens, the pits allow you to get nice and close. And because they are circular, groups can congregate around them, allowing many people to benefit at once. The pits even offer shelves where you can rest your beverage while watching the game. The smoldering logs are purely decorative; the flames are fueled by natural gas.

If you aren't sitting in the outfield and don't feel like taking a stroll to warm up beside one of the fire pits, you can still chase the chill from your bones by heading under the grandstand to the large fireplace on the concourse. Even walking past the hearth on your way to the bathroom or concession stands warms you up.

Of course, there are plenty of things worse in life than shivering through the final innings of a minor-league baseball game. We've all done it. But it sure is nice to see one team thought creatively and spent a few extra bucks to make our experience that much more enjoyable.

DOW DIAMOND

- Check out the **right field solar farm** that powers the ballpark scoreboard

- Visit the **Cove lounge**, which offers plush chairs and cocktails

- Play hopscotch on the **Midwest League map** at the park's right field playground

BALLPARK BUCKET LIST

The outfield fire pits provide places where fans can warm up on those chilly April nights.

High above the field,
fans watch a game
from the treetop seats.

THE TREETOP SEATS AT PARKVIEW FIELD

Glancing at a map, you might conclude Fort Wayne lies in a geographic no-team's-land when it comes to predicting residents' big-league rooting interests. After all, the city lies within a three-hour car ride from Detroit, Cleveland, Chicago, and Cincinnati. But make no mistake: Fort Wayne is Cubs country, even if the Midwest League TinCaps have been affiliated with the San Diego Padres since 1999. And the signature seating area at Parkview Field offers a tip of the (tin) cap to Wrigley Field.

Fort Wayne's Treetop Seats channel the spirit of the outfield roof decks from which Chicago fans have been peering into Wrigley for decades. The team's marketing materials even go so far as to proclaim, "Enjoy the Chicago Wrigley Field Rooftop experience right here in Fort Wayne," in describing the special seating area.

Nestled against the brick façade of the parking garage that abuts Parkview Field, the 250-seat deck does indeed resemble the seats overlooking Wrigley. And more than that, it offers excellent views of the field, while providing pavilion-style tables upon which you can rest your beverage and bag of peanuts while enjoying the game.

By virtue of their name, the Treetop Seats also honor American folk hero "Johnny Appleseed." Just as the TinCaps' name references the metal pot John Chapman wore on his head as he roamed the frontier planting seeds, the right field seats honor the trees Chapman adored. On March 18, 1845, Chapman passed away in Fort Wayne, but his memory lives on thanks to the city's annual Johnny Appleseed Festival held each September, and to the bush-league team and seats that honor his legacy.

So, order a bowl of Parkview Field's trademark apple crisp and enjoy a game from the Treetops!

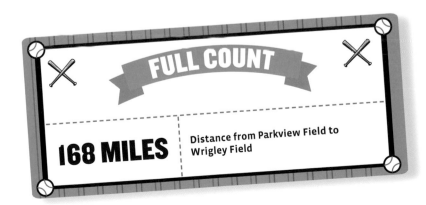

FULL COUNT

168 MILES | Distance from Parkview Field to Wrigley Field

Sugar Land Skeeters

THE TEXAS-SIZED SCOREBOARD AT CONSTELLATION FIELD

A visit to the southwest Houston suburb of Sugar Land allows you to gaze upon the unaffiliated minor leagues' most impressive scoreboard: a gigantic, Texas-shaped, high-definition board that rises 100 feet. It is as big as the boards you find in Triple-A, if not a little bigger, and towers over the field from its spot above the center field batter's eye. The thing that distinguishes the board even more than its size, though, is its framing. The screen is set within a giant silhouette of the state of Texas. This super-sized Lone Star State puzzle piece incorporates one hundred small LED panels that provide everything from player headshots, to statistics, to game highlights, to instant replays. If you're thinking you just don't find boards like this in the independent leagues, you're right! You ordinarily don't.

While most independent leagues offer a quality of play comparable to what you find in Class A of the affiliated minors, the Atlantic League is more competitive, falling somewhere between the Double-A and Triple-A levels, and its parks reflect that more advanced status. In fact, nearly half of the Atlantic League's players have spent time in the Bigs.

That said, it is an obvious step down for former big leaguers when they arrive in indy ball after toiling under the bright lights of the big leagues. But the erstwhile major leaguers in Sugar Land have no cause to gripe about their home park. The $37 million stadium sits beside the city's old Imperial Sugar refinery, treating fans and players to many creature comforts and design flourishes. The giant Texas scoreboard is what you remember most after heading home, though. The board is in your field of sight all game long and by virtue of its size and shape is quite arresting. Everything is bigger in Texas, indeed!

CONSTELLATION FIELD

- Take a selfie set against the park's regal **southwestern façade**

- Keep your eyes peeled for **Swatson**, the Skeeters' green mosquito mascot

- Visit the outfield **splash pad** or **swimming pool** to cool off

BALLPARK BUCKET LIST

The Texas-shaped scoreboard rises above the center field fence.

The Bobblehead Museum even includes bobbles modeled after baseball's mascots.

THE BOBBLEHEAD MUSEUM AT MARLINS PARK

Miami Marlins owner Jeffrey Loria made his fortune as an art dealer before entering the wild world of professional sports, and that passion for collecting led to his installing the world's largest assemblage of bobblehead dolls at Marlins Park. As you pass the Fan Feast stand on the park's promenade level, you come upon the two-sided display case dedicated to the little nodders that have been humoring us ever since papier-mâché wobblers portraying Mickey Mantle, Willie Mays, Roger Maris, and Roberto Clemente appeared in the 1960s.

The Bobblehead Museum includes bobbles depicting players, mascots, broadcasters, and other baseball personalities. American Leaguers appear on one side of the case, and National Leaguers on the other, sorted by team. Interior lighting allows you to study each of the bobbles in the 600 tiny compartments, and the shelves even vibrate so the heads on the dolls bobble. Among the notables are dolls of Mays, Randy Johnson, Willie McCovey, Tom Seaver, Fernando Valenzuela, and Robin Yount. The Mays piece captures the "Say Hey Kid" with his back turned to the plate and arms extended as he makes "The Catch" in the 1954 World Series.

The Marlins section includes a bobble portraying Craig Counsell pumping his fist in the air as he scores the winning run in Game Seven of the 1997 World Series, as well as bobbles of Marlins fan-favorites like Charles Johnson, Mike Lowell, Jeff Conine, Giancarlo Stanton, and Jose Fernandez.

The mascot section includes Mr. Met, the Phillie Phanatic, the San Diego Chicken, Bernie Brewer, and other ballpark pranksters.

 ## *Ballpark Chatter*

"They're fabulous little objects. They're sculptures. To me, they're works of art."

—JEFFREY LORIA, MARLINS OWNER

(Within each region, ballpark wonders are organized alphabetically by state.)

NEW ENGLAND

The Lighthouse at Hadlock Field
Portland Sea Dogs
271 Park Ave.
Portland, ME 04104

The Maine Monster at Hadlock Field
Portland Sea Dogs
271 Park Ave.
Portland, ME 04104

The Green Monster at Fenway Park
Boston Red Sox
4 Yawkey Way
Boston, MA 02215

The Red Seat at Fenway Park
Boston Red Sox
4 Yawkey Way
Boston, MA 02215

The Pesky Pole at Fenway Park
Boston Red Sox
4 Yawkey Way
Boston, MA 02215

The Wooden Grandstand Seats at Fenway Park
Boston Red Sox
4 Yawkey Way
Boston, MA 02215

The Outfield Hotel at Northeast Delta
   Dental Stadium
New Hampshire Fisher Cats
1 Line Dr.
Manchester, NH 03102

The Longest Game Exhibit at McCoy Stadium
Pawtucket Red Sox
1 Columbus Ave.
Pawtucket, RI 02860

The Player Portraits at McCoy Stadium
Pawtucket Red Sox
1 Columbus Ave.
Pawtucket, RI 02860

The Fishing Rails at McCoy Stadium
Pawtucket Red Sox
1 Columbus Ave.
Pawtucket, RI 02860

THE MID-ATLANTIC

The Racing Presidents at Nationals Park
Washington Nationals
1500 South Capitol St. SE
Washington, DC 20003

The B&O Warehouse at Oriole Park at Camden Yards
Baltimore Orioles
333 West Camden St.
Baltimore, MD 21201

Boog's Barbecue at Oriole Park at Camden Yards
Baltimore Orioles
333 West Camden St.
Baltimore, MD 21201

The Sun Sign at Oriole Park at Camden Yards
Baltimore Orioles
333 West Camden St.
Baltimore, MD 21201

The Lifeguard Chairs at FirstEnergy Park
Lakewood BlueClaws
2 Stadium Way
Lakewood, NJ 08701

The Frieze at Yankee Stadium
New York Yankees
1 E. 161st St.
Bronx, NY 10451

Monument Park at Yankee Stadium
New York Yankees
1 E. 161st St.
Bronx, NY 10451

Roll Call at Yankee Stadium
New York Yankees
1 E. 161st St.
Bronx, NY 10451

Shea Bridge at Citi Field
New York Mets
123-01 Roosevelt Ave.
New York, NY 11368

The Home Run Apple at Citi Field
New York Mets
123-01 Roosevelt Ave.
New York, NY 11368

The Jackie Robinson Rotunda at Citi Field
New York Mets
123-01 Roosevelt Ave.
New York, NY 11368

The Neon Skyline at MCU Park
Brooklyn Cyclones
1904 Surf Ave.
Brooklyn, NY 11224

The Giant Coke Bottle at Coca-Cola Park
Lehigh Valley IronPigs
1050 IronPigs Way
Allentown, PA 18109

The Roller Coaster at Peoples Natural Gas Field
Altoona Curve
1000 Park Ave.
Altoona, PA 16602

The Phillie Phanatic at Citizens Bank Park
Philadelphia Phillies
1 Citizens Bank Way
Philadelphia, PA 19148

The Liberty Bell at Citizens Bank Park
Philadelphia Phillies
1 Citizens Bank Way
Philadelphia, PA 19148

The Roberto Clemente Bridge at PNC Park
Pittsburgh Pirates
115 Federal St.
Pittsburgh, PA 15212

The Crazy Hot Dog Vendor at FirstEnergy Stadium
Reading Fightin Phils
1900 Centre Ave.
Reading, PA 19601

The Exploding Train Sign at FirstEnergy Stadium
Reading Fightin Phils
1900 Centre Ave.
Reading, PA 19601

THE SOUTH

The Train Shed at Montgomery Riverwalk Stadium
Montgomery Biscuits
200 Coosa St.
Montgomery, AL 36104

The Biscuits at Montgomery Riverwalk Stadium
Montgomery Biscuits
200 Coosa St.
Montgomery, AL 36104

The Green Monster Seats at JetBlue Park
Spring Home of the Boston Red Sox
11500 Fenway South Dr.
Fort Myers, FL 33913

The Aquatic Backstop at Marlins Park
Miami Marlins
501 Marlins Way
Miami, FL 33125

The Bobblehead Museum at Marlins Park
Miami Marlins
501 Marlins Way
Miami, FL 33125

The Home Run Sculpture at Marlins Park
Miami Marlins
501 Marlins Way
Miami, FL 33125

The Boardwalk at Charlotte Sports Park
Charlotte Stone Crabs and Spring Home of the
    Tampa Bay Rays
2300 El Jobean Rd.
Port Charlotte, FL 33948

The Rays Touch Tank at Tropicana Field
Tampa Bay Rays
1 Tropicana Dr.
St. Petersburg, FL 33705

The Snorting Bull at Durham Bulls Athletic Park
Durham Bulls
409 Blackwell St.
Durham, NC 27701

The Skyline at BB&T Ballpark
Charlotte Knights
324 S. Mint St.
Charlotte, NC 28202

The Nostalgia Man Statue at AutoZone Park
Memphis Redbirds
200 Union Ave.
Memphis, TN 38103

The Guitar Scoreboard at First Tennessee Park
Nashville Sounds
401 Jackson St.
Nashville, TN 37219

The Stone Castle at Calfee Park
Pulaski Yankees
700 S. Washington Ave.
Pulaski, VA 24301

Mini Fenway at Lewis-Gale Field at Salem Memorial
    Baseball Stadium
Salem Red Sox
1004 Texas St.
Salem, VA 24153

THE MIDWEST

The Ivy at Wrigley Field
Chicago Cubs
1060 West Addison St.
Chicago, IL 60613

The Rooftop Seats at Wrigley Field
Chicago Cubs
1060 West Addison St.
Chicago, IL 60613

The Scoreboard at Wrigley Field
Chicago Cubs
1060 West Addison St.
Chicago, IL 60613

The Bartman Seat at Wrigley Field
Chicago Cubs
1060 West Addison St.
Chicago, IL 60613

The Exploding Scoreboard at U.S. Cellular Field
Chicago White Sox
333 W. 35th St.
Chicago, IL 60616

The Statues at U.S. Cellular Field
Chicago White Sox
333 W. 35th St.
Chicago, IL 60616

The Racine Belles Signs at Bosse Field
Evansville Otters
23 Don Mattingly Way
Evansville, IN 47711

The Treetop Seats at Parkview Field
Fort Wayne TinCaps
1301 Ewing St.
Fort Wayne, IN 46802

The Left Field Curve at Ashford University Field
Clinton LumberKings
537 Ballpark Dr.
Clinton, IA 52732

The Giant Wheel at Modern Woodmen Park
Quad Cities River Bandits
209 S. Gaines St.
Davenport, IA 52802

The Water Fountain at Principal Park
Iowa Cubs
1 Line Dr.
Des Moines, IA 50309

The Outfield Statues at Comerica Park
Detroit Tigers
2100 Woodward Ave.
Detroit, MI 48201

The Prowling Tigers at Comerica Park
Detroit Tigers
2100 Woodward Ave.
Detroit, MI 48201

The Outfield Fire Pits at Dow Diamond
Great Lakes Loons
825 E. Main St.
Midland, MI 48640

The Beach House Façade at Wuerfel Park
Traverse City Beach Bums
333 Stadium Dr.
Traverse City, MI 49685

The Minnie and Paul Sign at Target Field
Minnesota Twins
1 Twins Way
Minneapolis, MN 55403

The Yellow Limestone at Target Field
Minnesota Twins
1 Twins Way
Minneapolis, MN 55403

The Funky Seats at CHS Field
St. Paul Saints
360 North Broadway
St. Paul, MN 55101

The Water Spectacular at Kauffman Stadium
Kansas City Royals
1 Royal Way
Kansas City, MO 64129

The Buck O'Neil Legacy Seat at Kauffman Stadium
Kansas City Royals
1 Royal Way
Kansas City, MO 64129

The Crown Scoreboard at Kauffman Stadium
Kansas City Royals
1 Royal Way
Kansas City, MO 64129

The Gateway Arch at Busch Stadium
St. Louis Cardinals
700 Clark St.
St. Louis, MO 63102

The Riverboat and Power Stacks at Great American
   Ball Park
Cincinnati Reds
100 Joe Nuxhall Way
Cincinnati, OH 45202

The Drummer at Progressive Field
Cleveland Indians
2401 Ontario St.
Cleveland, OH 44115

#TribeLive at Progressive Field
Cleveland Indians
2401 Ontario St.
Cleveland, OH 44115

The Smoking Dragons at Fifth Third Field
Dayton Dragons
220 N. Patterson Blvd.
Dayton, OH 45402

The Hotel Rooms at Rogers Centre
Toronto Blue Jays
One Blue Jays Way
Toronto, Ontario M5V 1J
Canada

The Sausage Race at Miller Park
Milwaukee Brewers
One Brewers Way
Milwaukee, WI 53214

THE SOUTHWEST

The Ziz at Goodyear Ballpark
Spring Home of the Cincinnati Reds and Cleveland
    Indians
1933 S. Ballpark Way
Goodyear, AZ 85338

The Swimming Pool at Chase Field
Arizona Diamondbacks
401 E. Jefferson St.
Phoenix, AZ 85004

The Keyhole at Chase Field
Arizona Diamondbacks
401 E. Jefferson St.
Phoenix, AZ 85004

The Desert Setting of Camelback Ranch–Glendale
Spring Home of the Los Angeles Dodgers and
    Chicago White Sox
10710 W. Camelback Rd.
Phoenix, AZ 85037

The Simpsons Statues at Isotopes Park
Albuquerque Isotopes
1601 Avenida Cesar Chavez Southeast
Albuquerque, NM 87106

The Outfield Slope at Isotopes Park
Albuquerque Isotopes
1601 Avenida Cesar Chavez Southeast
Albuquerque, NM 87106

The Oil Derrick at ONEOK Field
Tulsa Drillers
201 N. Elgin Ave.
Tulsa, OK 74120

Greene's Hill at Globe Life Park in Arlington
Texas Rangers
1000 Ballpark Way
Arlington, TX 76011

The Cotton Presses at Whataburger Field
Corpus Christi Hooks
734 E. Port Ave.
Corpus Christi, TX 78401

The Right Field Towers at Southwest
    University Park
El Paso Chihuahuas
1 Ballpark Plaza
El Paso, TX 79901

The Lazy River at Dr Pepper Ballpark
Frisco RoughRiders
7300 RoughRiders Trail
Frisco, TX 75034

The Steam Train at Minute Maid Park
Houston Astros
501 Crawford St.
Houston, TX 77002

The Texas-Sized Scoreboard at Constellation Field
Sugar Land Skeeters
1 Stadium Dr.
Sugar Land, TX 77498

THE WEST

The Big A at Angel Stadium of Anaheim
Los Angeles Angels of Anaheim
2000 Gene Autry Way
Anaheim, CA 92806

The California Spectacular at Angel Stadium
    of Anaheim
Los Angeles Angels of Anaheim
2000 Gene Autry Way
Anaheim, CA 92806

The Wavy Roofs at Dodger Stadium
Los Angeles Dodgers
1000 Elysian Park Ave.
Los Angeles, CA 90090

The Bleacher Diehards at Oakland Coliseum
Oakland Athletics
7000 Coliseum Way
Oakland, CA 94621

The Beach at Petco Park
San Diego Padres
19 Tony Gwynn Way
San Diego, CA 92101

The Western Metal Supply Company Building
    at Petco Park
San Diego Padres
19 Tony Gwynn Way
San Diego, CA 92101

The Cable Car at AT&T Park
San Francisco Giants
24 Willie Mays Plaza
San Francisco, CA 94107

The Giant Glove at AT&T Park
San Francisco Giants
24 Willie Mays Plaza
San Francisco, CA 94107

Levi's Landing at AT&T Park
San Francisco Giants
24 Willie Mays Plaza
San Francisco, CA 94107

The Red Barn at Rawhide Ballpark
Visalia Rawhide
300 N. Giddings St.
Visalia, CA 93291

The Mile High Seats at Coors Field
Colorado Rockies
2001 Blake St.
Denver, CO 80205

The Outfield Forest at Coors Field
Colorado Rockies
2001 Blake St.
Denver, CO 80205

The Mountain Views at Smith's Ballpark
Salt Lake Bees
77 W. 1300 South
Salt Lake City, UT 84115

The Roof at Safeco Field
Seattle Mariners
1250 First Ave. South
Seattle, WA 98134

The Ben Cheney Statue at Cheney Stadium
Tacoma Rainiers
2502 S. Tyler St.
Tacoma, WA 98405

TRAVELING BALLPARK WONDERS

The San Diego Chicken
Coming to a Ballpark Near You

The ZOOperstars!
Coming to a Ballpark Near You

Frontispiece photo, see chapter 3

Title page photo, see chapter 9

Photos opposite copyright page, top: see chapter 37; middle: see chapter 4; bottom: see chapter 98

Introduction
Frieze at Yankee Stadium, see chapter 8; Durham Bull, see chapter 1; Josh Pahigian author photo with son Spencer, Photo by Josh Pahigian; Marlins Park bobbleheads, see chapter 101; Monument Park at Yankee Stadium, see chapter 13; The Big A, see chapter 20

1. The Snorting Bull at Durham Bulls Athletic Park
Bull closeup from Durham Bulls, Courtesy of Brian Fleming; full bull from Durham Bulls, Courtesy of Brian Fleming; The Durham Bull (center photo), Courtesy of the Durham Convention & Visitors Bureau, https://durham.webdamdb.com

2. The Crazy Hot Dog Vendor at FirstEnergy Stadium
All photos Courtesy of Tug Haines/ Reading Fightin Phils

3. The Sausage Race at Miller Park
Sausage Race closeup, Courtesy of Dan Eidsmoe; Sausage Race, Photo Courtesy of David Rogers; Sausage Race, Courtesy of the Milwaukee Brewers Baseball Club

Blast from the Past: Max Patkin, The Clown Prince of Baseball
All photos Courtesy of the National Baseball Hall of Fame Library, Cooperstown, NY

4. The Green Monster at Fenway Park
Green Monster closeup, Flickr Commons photo by Doug Kerr, www.flickr.com/photos/dougtone/9192907460; Fenway at twilight, photo by Josh Pahigian; Green Monster, US Navy Public Domain Photo, US Air Force photo by Rick Berry

5. The San Diego Chicken
San Diego Chicken biting fan, Photo by Ben Horne; San Diego Chicken with baby chicks, Photo by Tony Amat; San Diego Chicken with umpire, Photo by Tony Amat

6. The Ivy at Wrigley Field
Wrigley ivy, Flickr Commons photo by Aaron Porzel, www.flickr.com/photos/aaronporzel/13645538345

7. The Phillie Phanatic at Citizens Bank Park
Phillie Phanatic, Flickr Commons Photo by Arturo Pardavila III, www.flickr.com/photos/apardavila/19311083025

8. The Frieze at Yankee Stadium
Yankee Stadium frieze closeup, Flickr Commons photo by Steven Pisano, https://www.flickr.com/photos/stevenpisano/18091435521; Yankee Stadium frieze, photo by Josh Pahigian

9. The Roberto Clemente Bridge at PNC Park
Clemente Bridge, bridge view, Flickr Commons photo by Roy Luck; www.flickr.com/photos/21550937@N03/8759717450; Clemente Bridge, Courtesy of David Rogers

10. The Guitar Scoreboard at First Tennessee Park
Guitar scoreboard with Hamilton on board, Courtesy of Nashville Sounds/Mike Strasinger; old guitar scoreboard from Greer Stadium, Wikimedia Commons Photo by Brent Moore, https://commons.wikimedia.org/wiki/File:GreerStadiumScoreboard2.jpg

11. The Racing Presidents at Nationals Park
Abe Lincoln at Nationals Park, Flickr Commons Photo by Eric Kilby, www.flickr.com/photos/ekilby/2866464091; Presidents Race wide view, Flickr Commons Photo by Eric Kilby, www.flickr.com/photos/ekilby/2866461967

12. The Jackie Robinson Rotunda at Citi Field
Jackie Robinson Rotunda, Flickr Commons Photo by iamNigelMorris, www.flickr.com/photos/34639903@N03/3436404991; Jackie Robinson Memorial, Wikimedia Commons Photo by Jtesla16, https://commons.wikimedia.org/wiki/File:Jackie_Robinson_Memorial.JPG

13. Monument Park at Yankee Stadium
Monument Park, Photo Courtesy of Kathryn Kolodziej; Monument Park retired numbers, Flickr Commons Photo by Arturo Pardavila III, www.flickr.com/photos/apardavila/21295505378

14. The Smoking Dragons at Fifth Third Field
Dragons scoreboard in Dayton, Courtesy of the Dayton Dragons

15. The Water Spectacular at Kauffman Stadium
Kauffman Fountains closeup, Courtesy of David Rogers; Kauffman Stadium fountain view, Flickr Commons photo by David Fulmer, www.flickr.com/photos/daveynin/5872896143

Blast from the Past: Hot Pants Day, Oakland A's, June 27, 1971
Photos by Ron Riesterer/PhotoShelter

16. The ZOOperstars!
ZOOperstars, Photos by Karen Naess

17. The Wavy Roofs at Dodger Stadium
Dodger Stadium roof, Courtesy of Gary Paul Smith; Dodger Stadium outfield view, Wikimedia Commons, https://commons.wikimedia.org/wiki/File:Dodger_Stadium_field_from_upper_deck_2015-10-04.jpg

18. The Simpsons Statues at Isotopes Park
Both photos Courtesy of MOJI Photography/Albuquerque Isotopes

19. The Home Run Apple at Citi Field
Mets Home Run Apple distant, Photo by Josh Pahigian; Home Run Apple closeup, Flickr Commons photo by Marianne O'Leary, www.flickr.com/photos/marianne_oleary/5897187144;
original Home Run Apple, Photo by Josh Pahigian

20. The Big A at Angel Stadium of Anaheim
Wikimedia Commons Photo by Nandaro, https://commons.wikimedia.org/wiki/File:20140702-0183_Angel_Stadium.jpg

21. The Giant Wheel at Modern Woodmen Park
Both photos Courtesy of Scott D. Peterson

22. The Drummer at Progressive Field
Indians Drummer John Adams, Photo Courtesy of David Goodman; John Adams crowd shot, Photo by David Rogers

23. The Swimming Pool at Chase Field
Both photos Courtesy of the Arizona Diamondbacks

24. The Exploding Scoreboard at U.S. Cellular Field
Flickr Commons Photo by Barry D, www.flickr.com/photos/jjway2006/3893430251

25. The Nostalgia Man Statue at AutoZone Park
Flickr Commons Photo by Ron Cogswell, www.flickr.com/photos/22711505@N05/8529788270

26. The Outfield Statues at Comerica Park
Comerica Park Statues, Photo Courtesy of David Rogers; Ty Cobb statue, Flickr Commons Photo by Dave Hogg, www.flickr.com/photos/davehogg/538157370

27. The Red Seat at Fenway Park
All photos by Josh Pahigian

Blast from the Past: The Rockford Peaches, The All-American Girls Professional Baseball League, 1943–1954
Photos Courtesy of the National Baseball Hall of Fame Library, Cooperstown, NY

28. The Desert Setting at Camelback Ranch–Glendale
Camelback Ranch grandstand view, Wikimedia Commons Photo by Nick Panico, https://commons.wikimedia.org/wiki/File:Camelback_Ranch_view_from_right_field.jpg; Camelback Ranch right field mountain view, Photo by Josh Pahigian; Camelback Ranch scoreboard, Flickr Commons Photo by John Verive, www.flickr.com/photos/octopushat/4415521493

29. The Bleacher Diehards at Oakland Coliseum
Both photos Courtesy of Chip Scarinzi

30. The Neon Skyline at MCU Park
MCU Park scoreboard and neon light towers, Flickr Commons Photo by Gene Han, www.flickr.com/photos/larimdame/311830; Parachute Jump at MCU Park, Flickr Commons Photo by Eden, Janine, and Jim, www.flickr.com/photos/edenpictures/14529015424

31. The Liberty Bell at Citizens Bank Park
Liberty Bell at Citizens Bank Park, Wikimedia Commons photo by minimoniotaku, https://commons.wikimedia.org/wiki/File:S8000749.JPG

32. The Roof at Safeco Field
The roof at Safeco Field, Public Domain, https://pixabay.com/en/seattle-safeco-field-stadium-277120

33. The Cotton Presses at Whataburger Field
Both photos Courtesy of Corpus Christi Hooks/Amanda Pruett

34. The Gateway Arch at Busch Stadium
Gateway Arch closeup, Photo Courtesy of David Rogers; St. Louis Arch, Photo Courtesy of Amanda Markel

35. The Lazy River at Dr Pepper Ballpark
Photos Courtesy of the Frisco RoughRiders

36. The Scoreboard at Wrigley Field
Wrigley scoreboard, Flickr Commons Photo by joenevill, www.flickr.com/photos/joenevill/14479966955; Wrigley scoreboard with pennants, Wikimedia Commons Photo by TonyTheTiger, https://commons.wiki media.org/wiki/File:201200801_Wrigley_Field_scoreboard.JPG

37. The Minnie and Paul Sign at Target Field
Minnie and Paul at night, Courtesy of David Rogers; Minnie and Paul closeup, Flickr Commons photo by Shilad Sen, www.flickr.com/photos/41471683@N00/4630573311

38. The Mile High Seats at Coors Field
Mile High Seats, Flickr Commons Photo by Hey Paul, www.flickr.com/photos/heypaul/2557123951; Mile High Seats 2, Courtesy of Eric Lo

39. The Longest Game Exhibit at McCoy Stadium
Photos by Josh Pahigian

Blast from the Past: The Lights at Crosley Field, Cincinnati Reds, May 24, 1935
Photo Courtesy of the National Baseball Hall of Fame Library, Cooperstown, NY

40. The Hotel Rooms at Rogers Centre
Views from the hotel, Two Photos Courtesy of David A. Kelly; Exterior shot, Flickr Commons Photo by Christine K, www.flickr.com/photos/lam_chihang/6062051846

41. The B&O Warehouse at Oriole Park at Camden Yards
Flickr Commons Photo by Keith Allison, www.flickr.com/photos/keithallison/8918202788 and www.flickr .com/photos/keithallison/18787357692

42. The Lighthouse at Hadlock Field
Lighthouse, Photo by Josh Pahigian; Exploding Lighthouse, Photo Courtesy of the Portland Sea Dogs

43. The Crown Scoreboard at Kauffman Stadium
Crown scoreboard, Photo Courtesy of Mike Day; back of Royals scoreboard, Photo Courtesy of David Rogers

44. The Rooftop Seats at Wrigley Field
Wrigley rooftop view, Flickr Commons photo by Grant Wickes, www.flickr.com/photos/grantwickes/ 14358415862

45. The Pesky Pole at Fenway Park
Photos by Josh Pahigian

46. The Steam Train at Minute Maid Park
Photos Courtesy of the Houston Astros

47. The Red Barn at Rawhide Ballpark
Photos Courtesy of Chris Henstra

48. The Oil Derrick at ONEOK Field
Photos Courtesy of the Tulsa Drillers

49. The Mountain Views at Smith's Ballpark
Photo Courtesy of Brent Asay/Salt Lake Bees

50. Greene's Hill at Globe Life Park in Arlington
Greene's Hill, Flickr Commons Photo by theterrifictc, www.flickr.com/photos/theterrifictc/3783823904; Greene's Hill with Texas National Guard, Flickr Commons Photo by Texas Military Forces Staff Sgt. Eric Wilson, www.flickr.com/photos/texasmilitaryforces/6277122552

51. The Wooden Grandstand Seats at Fenway Park
Photos by Josh Pahigian

Blast from the Past: Seals Stadium, Major League Baseball's First West Coast Game, April 15, 1958
Photos Courtesy of the Associated Press

52. The Outfield Forest at Coors Field
Center field forest wide view, Flickr Commons Photo by Thomas, www.flickr.com/photos/photommo/9146463706; Coors Field geyser, Photo Courtesy of Gary Paul Smith

53. The Beach at Petco Park
Two Photos Courtesy of Chip Scarinzi; Sand Sculpture, Flickr Commons Photo by Peyri Herrera, www.flickr.com/photos/peyri/6321720180/

54. The Keyhole at Chase Field
Photos Courtesy of the Arizona Diamondbacks

55. The Funky Seats at CHS Field
Photos Courtesy of St. Paul Saints/Christy Radecic

56. The Cable Car at AT&T Park
Giants Cable Car game view, © 2015 S.F. Giants; Giants Cable Car 2, Photo Courtesy of Jamison Wieser

57. The Fishing Rails at McCoy Stadium
Photos by Josh Pahigian

58. The Riverboat and Power Stacks at Great American Ball Park
The Riverboat and Power Stacks, Photo Courtesy of David Rogers; Riverboat in Center Field, Flickr Commons Photo by Daniel Betts, www.flickr.com/photos/redlegsfan21/22645007984

59. The Rays Touch Tank at Tropicana Field
Photos Courtesy of Jodi Petrinovich

60. The Giant Coke Bottle at Coca-Cola Park
Coca-Cola Park, Flickr Commons Photo by Doug Kerr, www.flickr.com/photos/dougtone/9343056526; Coca-Cola wide shot side view, Photo Courtesy of Digital Photographic Imaging

61. The Green Monster Seats at JetBlue Park
Pregame JetBlue Monster, Photo by Josh Pahigian; game-time JetBlue Monster, Wikimedia Commons Photo by NT1952, https://commons.wikimedia.org/wiki/File:JetBlue_Park_at_Fenway_South.JPG

62. The Lifeguard Chairs at FirstEnergy Park
Lakewood FirstEnergy Park wide view, Wikimedia Commons Photo by KOknockout920, https://en.wikipedia.org/wiki/FirstEnergy_Park#/media/File:Firstenergyparklakewood.JPG; Lakewood Lifeguard Chairs, Photo Courtesy of Zach Binney, Ben Carroll, Pat Lange, Scrappyjourneymenwithheart.blogspot.com

63. The Yellow Limestone at Target Field
Target Field left field view, Flicker Commons Photo by Jonathan Miske, www.flickr.com/photos/jmiske/20740156306; Target Field, Wikimedia Commons Photo in Public Domain, https://commons.wikimedia.org/wiki/File:140715-F-PM992-070_Thunderbirds_perform_the_MLB_All-Star_Game_flyover.JPG

Blast from the Past: Greenlee Field, Pittsburgh Crawfords, 1932–1938
Photos Courtesy of the National Baseball Hall of Fame Library, Cooperstown, NY

64. Shea Bridge at Citi Field
Photos by Josh Pahigian

65. The Skyline at BB&T Ballpark
Photo Courtesy of Laura Wolff/Charlotte Knights

66. The Aquatic Backstop at Marlins Park
Soriano and Castro photos, Photos Courtesy of Miguel A. Sanchez; Marlins Park fish tank, Flickr Commons Photo by Steve, www.flickr.com/photos/mrlaugh/7793670838

67. The California Spectacular at Angel Stadium of Anaheim
Flickr Commons Photo by Ray S, www.flickr.com/photos/15132846@N00/5651019539; Eric Hinske photo by Amin Eshaiker, own work, CC BY-SA 3.0, http://bit.ly/2davG6t

68. The Western Metal Supply Company Building at Petco Park
Western Metal Supply Co Building with Sailors, Flickr Commons photo by Naval Surface Warriors, www.flickr.com/photos/navalsurfaceforces/19363892071; Western Metal Supply, Flickr Commons photo by Eric Golub, www.flickr.com/photos/sirqitous/17173335785

69. The Outfield Slope at Isotopes Park
Outfield hill wider view, Photo courtesy of Matt Locke; outfield hill close-up Courtesy Albuquerque Isotopes; Isotopes Park outfield view, Flickr Commons Photo by littlemoresunshine, www.flickr.com/photos/littlemoresunshine/10394088224

70. Roll Call at Yankee Stadium
Yankee Bleacher Creatures, David Wells, Flickr Commons Photo by Chris Ptacek, www.flickr.com/photos/chrisptacek/3449283138; Yankee Stadium right field bleachers, Photo by Josh Pahigian

71. The Prowling Tigers at Comerica Park
Comerica Prowling Tigers at entrance, Wikimedia Commons Photo by Keropian, https://commons.wikimedia.org/wiki/File:Comerica_Park_North_Gate.jpg; Comerica Park scoreboard Tiger, Wikimedia Commons Photo by Kevin Ward, https://commons.wikimedia.org/wiki/File:Tiger_Statue_of_Comerica_Park.jpg; Comerica Tiger closeup, Flickr Commons Photo by Michael Kumm, www.flickr.com/photos/mkumm/2448937313; giant Tigers with Comerica Park sign, Flickr Commons Photo by Grangernite, www.flickr.com/photos/ldoty/1549017764

72. The Giant Glove at AT&T Park
Photos © 2015 S.F. Giants

73. Boog's Barbecue at Oriole Park at Camden Yards
Boog Powell at his stand, Flickr Commons Photo by Navin Rajagopalan, www.flickr.com/photos/navin75/9318545156; Boog Powell first pitch, Flickr Commons Photo by Keith Allison, www.flickr.com/photos/27003603@N00/2417156946; Boog Powell chatting, Photo by Josh Pahigian

74. The Player Portraits at McCoy Stadium
Photos by Josh Pahigian

75. The Roller Coaster at Peoples Natural Gas Field
Altoona Coaster, Wikimedia Commons Photo by MightyRoach, https://commons.wikimedia.org/wiki/File:Field_at_BCB.JPG

Blast from the Past: The Polo Grounds' Cavernous Center Field, 1883–1963
Polo Grounds game, Photo Courtesy of the Library of Congress; 475-feet marker, Photo Courtesy of the National Baseball Hall of Fame Library, Cooperstown, NY

76. The Outfield Hotel at Northeast Delta Dental Stadium
Photos by Josh Pahigian

77. The Ben Cheney Statue at Cheney Stadium
Photo Courtesy Red Williamson/Tacoma Rainiers

78. The Exploding Train Sign at FirstEnergy Stadium
Photos Courtesy of Matt Jackson/Reading Fightin Phils

79. The Maine Monster at Hadlock Field
Photos by Josh Pahigian

80. The Buck O'Neil Legacy Seat at Kauffman Stadium
Wikimedia Commons, Public Domain photo, https://commons.wikimedia.org/wiki/File:BuckONeilLegacySeat2009.jpg

81. The Train Shed at Montgomery Riverwalk Stadium
Photo by Josh Pahigian

82. The Home Run Sculpture at Marlins Park
Home Run Sculpture, Flickr Commons Photo by Dan Lundberg, https://www.flickr.com/photos/9508280@N07/6942957678; Home Run Sculpture lights, Flickr Commons Photo by Jared, www.flickr.com/photos/jared422/8772283985

83. The Statues at U.S. Cellular Field
Carlton Fisk statue, Flickr Commons Photo by Bryce Edwards; www.flickr.com/photos/bryce_edwards/10483763863; Harold Baines statue, Flickr Commons Photo by Bryce Edwards, www.flickr.com/photos/bryce_edwards/10483961476

84. The Stone Castle at Calfee Park
Photos Courtesy of Jade Campbell

85. The Racine Belles Signs at Bosse Field
Photo Courtesy of Andrea Wallace

86. The Boardwalk at Charlotte Sports Park
Baseball Boardwalk, Photo by Josh Pahigian; Baseball Boardwalk sign, Flickr Commons Photo by Don Johnson 395, www.flickr.com/photos/donjohnson395/3296158562; boardwalk with fans, Flickr Commons Photo by Don Johnson 395, www.flickr.com/photos/donjohnson395/3379434993

87. Levi's Landing at AT&T Park
Photos © 2015 S.F. Giants

Blast from the Past: Elysian Fields, Hoboken, New Jersey, October 1859
Illustration Courtesy of the Library of Congress

88. Mini Fenway at Lewis-Gale Field at Salem Memorial Baseball Stadium
Photos Courtesy of Samantha Barney

89. The Water Fountain at Principal Park
Photos Courtesy of Ellie Walter/Iowa Cubs

90. The Beach House Façade at Wuerfel Park
Photo Courtesy of Michael D. Burrill

91. The Bartman Seat at Wrigley Field
Wikimedia Commons Public Domain Photo, https://en.wikipedia.org/wiki/File:Bartman_seat_heckler.jpg

92. *The Ziz* at Goodyear Ballpark
Photo Courtesy of Donald Lipski

93. The Left Field Curve at Ashford University Field
Photos Courtesy of the Clinton Lumber Kings Baseball Club

94. #TribeLive at Progressive Field
Photo Courtesy of Megan Gruttadaurio

95. The Biscuits at Montgomery Riverwalk Stadium
Photo Courtesy of Steven P. Ericson

96. The Right Field Towers at Southwest University Park
Photos Courtesy of Ivan Pierre Aguirre, El Paso Chihuahuas

97. The Sun Sign at Oriole Park at Camden Yards
Flickr Commons photo by Keith Allison, www.flickr.com/photos/keithallison/8751036396

98. The Outfield Fire Pits at Dow Diamond
Photos Courtesy of Great Lakes Loons, Matt DeVries

99. The Treetop Seats at Parkview Field
Photos Courtesy of the Fort Wayne TinCaps

100. The Texas-Sized Scoreboard at Constellation Field
Constellation Field, Flickr Commons Photo by Roy Luck, www.flickr.com/photos/royluck/14288595427/in/photolist-fsEf1M-bXYVv5-nLCMBz-aqyxKt; Constellation Field scoreboard, Photo Courtesy of the Sugar Land Skeeters; Constellation scoreboard at night, Photo Courtesy of the Sugar Land Skeeters

101. The Bobblehead Museum at Marlins Park
Bobble Museum mascots, Flickr Commons Photo by slgckgc, https://www.flickr.com/photos/slgc/6935625470; Bobblehead Museum with fans, Photo Courtesy of David A. Kelly; Bobblehead Museum 3, Flickr Commons Photo by Jared, https://www.flickr.com/photos/jared422/8778832622

Author Photo by Heather Pahigian

Acknowledgments

As always, I extend my love and thanks to my friends and family members who support my writing, especially my wife Heather and children Spencer and Lauren. My parents and in-laws have also been extraordinarily generous in spreading the word about my books and buying copies of them for their friends, as well: my thanks to Richard and Cathy Pahigian, Judy and Ed Gurrie, Butch Razoyk and Lynn Pastor, and my brother Jamie.

I also owe a special debt of gratitude to my literary agent at the Doe Coover Agency, Colleen Mohyde, who has been with me since the beginning. As the years have passed, I've realized more and more what a grand slam I hit when I hooked on with Colleen and the other pros at Doe Coover. For being more than just a business associate, but a friend, sounding board, and, occasional life coach, thanks Colleen.

For believing in this book and giving it a life in print, I thank my editor at the Lyons Press, Keith Wallman, with whom I have had the pleasure of working on several projects now. For sticking with me, bouncing ideas around, and sharing in my love of the game, thanks Keith.

Finally, I would not have been able to complete this book without the contributions of the many people who have fielded my questions about their ballparks, have led me through their grounds, and have supported my efforts in other ways. My thanks to all the ballpark staffers and team executives who have lent a helping hand. I also could not have produced the book without the contributions of friends, old and new, who met up with me over several summers so that I wouldn't have to travel alone, who snapped photos at my side or in my absence, and who passed along their local knowledge of ballpark attractions so that I could incorporate it into the book. I thank Sean Aaronson, David Barac, Robbin Barnes, Samantha Barnes, Nathan Barnett, Zach Binney, Joe Bird, Chris Cameron, Jade Campbell, Ben Carroll, Brian Carroll, Matt Chisholm, Mike Day, Tony DesPlaines, Steven Ericson, Ted Giannoulas, Greg Giombarrese, Bruce Gobi, David Goodman, George Gratto, Jason Heid, Blair Hoke, Jake Holtrop, Matt Jackson, David A. Kelly, Kathryn Kolodziej, Pat Lange, Dominic Latkovski, Donald Lipski, Scott Litle, Eric Lo, Matt Locke, Jay Lucas, Amanda Markel, Paul R. Michaels, Suzanna Mitchell, Greg Mroz, Tom Nichols, Kevin O'Connell, Jennifer Pendergraft, Gil Perez, Jodi and Jack Petrinovich, Amanda Pruett, David Rogers, Matt Rogers, Miguel Sanchez, Chip Scarinzi, Chad Seely, Tom Seidler, Gary Paul Smith, Chris Stagno, Matt Sutor, John Traub, Tommy Viola, Andrea Wallace, Jason Webber, Jamison Wieser, Casey Wilcox, and Kraig Williams.

About the Author

Josh Pahigian spent his childhood and a little bit too much of his adolescence planning on one day being the third baseman for the Boston Red Sox. After batting .240 for the Shepherd Hill Regional High School junior varsity baseball team as a sophomore, he realized he needed a Plan B, which led to his majoring in English at the College of the Holy Cross and covering high school and college sports for the *Worcester Telegram & Gazette*. Later, while finishing a master of fine arts degree in creative writing at Emerson College, Josh and classmate Kevin O'Connell hatched a plan to convince a publisher to pay for their dream trip around the big leagues. To their delight, the scheme worked, and the product of their travels became *The Ultimate Baseball Road Trip* (Lyons Press). That book's success helped Josh land a gig as a recurring columnist for ESPN.com and led to future baseball books like *101 Baseball Places to See Before You Strike Out*, *The Seventh Inning Stretch,* and *The Ultimate Minor League Baseball Road Trip*, all with Lyons Press. After more than a decade spent writing about the baseball landscape, Josh received a legislative commendation from the Commonwealth of Massachusetts' House of Representatives in 2015 for his "commitment to preserving the history of America's favorite pastime."

Josh is also an accomplished fiction writer, having penned a critically acclaimed mystery novel titled *Strangers on the Beach*, and several short stories revealing the Armenian-American cultural experience that have been published in US literary journals and in translation in Armenia.

When he's not sitting at a ballpark or at his writing desk, Josh can be found teaching at the University of New England or Western Connecticut State University, or at the beach with his wife Heather, and children Spencer and Lauren.

Josh welcomes correspondence from readers, who may email him at pahigian35@ yahoo.com. Please also feel free to share the details of your own baseball adventures with Josh and fellow travelers on the Facebook page for this book at www.facebook.com/Amazing BaseballAdventure.

Josh Pahigian and Hadlock Field